REPORT TO CONGRESS ON THE "REVIEW OF FEDERAL AND STATE LAWS REGARDING VEHICLE TOWING"

May 2007

Prepared For:
Federal Motor Carrier Safety Administration
Vehicle and Roadside Operations Division
MC-PSV
400 7th Street, SW
Washington, DC 20590

Prepared By:
John A. Volpe National Transportation
Systems Center
Motor Carrier Safety Division
RTV-3E
55 Broadway
Cambridge, MA 02142

Technical Report Documentation Page

1. Report No.	2. Government Accession No.	3. Recipient's Catalog No.
4. Title and Subtitle Report to Congress on the "Review of Federal and State Laws Regarding Vehicle Towing"		**5. Report Date** May 21, 2007
		6. Performing Organization Code
7. Author(s)		**8. Performing Organization Report No.**
9. Performing Organization Name and Address U.S. Department of Transportation Research and Innovative Technology Administration John A. Volpe National Transportation Systems Center Motor Carrier Safety Division (RTV-3E) 55 Broadway Cambridge, MA 02142-1093		**10. Work Unit No. (TRAIS)**
		11. Contract or Grant No.
12. Sponsoring Agency Name and Address U.S. Department of Transportation Federal Motor Carrier Safety Administration Vehicle and Roadside Operations Division (MC-PSV) 400 7th Street, SW Washington, DC 20590		**13. Type of Report and Period Covered** Final Report
		14. Sponsoring Agency Code

15. Supplementary Notes:
Project Manager: Jeffrey Van Ness, Federal Motor Carrier Safety Administration

16. Abstract

This report summarizes current federal and state law and jurisprudence regarding nonconsensual motor vehicle towing, and also provides an overview of information obtained from major stakeholder groups regarding this topic. Major issues related to nonconsensual towing are highlighted, and some potential remedies to the problems identified are discussed.

17. Key Words Vehicle towing, nonconsensual towing, predatory towing, trespass towing, private property impound (PPI) towing		18. Distribution Statement		
19. Security Classif. (of this report) Unclassified	20. Security Classif. (of this page) Unclassified		21. No. of Pages 52	22. Price

Form DOT F 1700.7 (8-72)   **Reproduction of completed page authorized**

Acronym List

AAA: American Automobile Association
ATA: American Trucking Associations
ATowA: American Towing Alliance
CMR: Code of Massachusetts Regulations
DC: District of Columbia
FAAA: Federal Aviation Administration Authorization Act
FMCSA: Federal Motor Carrier Safety Administration
GPSC: Georgia Public Service Commission
ICCTA: Interstate Commerce Commission Termination Act of 1995
MGL: Massachusetts General Laws
NTRA: National Towing and Recovery Association
OOIDA: Owner-Operator Independent Drivers Association
PPI: Private Property Impound
SAFETEA-LU: Safe, Accountable, Flexible, Efficient Transportation Equity Act: A Legacy for Users
TRAA: Towing and Recovery Association of America
USC: United States Code

Table of Contents

List of Tables

Executive Summary

There are various circumstances under which vehicle towing services can be "nonconsensual," including the removal of an unauthorized vehicle from private property and the police-ordered removal of a vehicle for safety reasons. Because these situations present the vehicle owner with no opportunity to negotiate prices and terms for the towing service, nonconsensual towing fees are often regulated by States and localities to prevent unfair pricing and provide consumer protection. However, some of these protections have been interpreted through Court decisions to be preempted by Federal motor carrier law. More broadly, the rights of motorists whose vehicles have been towed without their consent are subject to a complex interaction between Federal, State, and local law.

Section 4105 of the most recent Federal transportation re-authorization bill, the Safe, Accountable, Flexible, Efficient Transportation Equity Act: A Legacy for Users (SAFETEA-LU) (P.L. 109-59), modified the legal framework in this area by granting additional authority to the States to regulate nonconsensual tows from private property. Section 4105 of SAFETEA-LU also requires the Secretary of Transportation to conduct a study to identify additional means to protect the rights of individuals whose motor vehicles are towed. This study addresses this question through an analysis of current Federal and State law and jurisprudence, along with consultation with major stakeholder groups.

In brief, this report finds that two Federal laws passed in the 1990s to deregulate the motor carrier industry also included provisions preempting State and local laws related to the prices, routes, and services of motor carriers, including towing services. However, there were several exceptions to this rule, including a specific statutory exemption for State laws related to the "price of" nonconsensual tows from private property and a broader exception for State regulations related to safety. Courts have differed in their decisions as to how broadly to interpret the "safety" exception, causing considerable uncertainty about the extent to which State regulation is federally preempted. Courts have also generally recognized a distinction between regulation and mere participation in the marketplace on the part of a State or locality.

This report also provides a review and analysis of State laws related to nonconsensual vehicle towing, drawing on a sample of nine States and the District of Columbia in order to assess the impact of State laws on the rights of motorists. All of the jurisdictions reviewed in this study regulate nonconsensual towing in some way, most commonly via requirements about the posting of notices on private property, the establishment of price ceilings on towing and storage charges, requirements for police notification, and regulations on the location and operation of the vehicle storage and reclaim facilities used in connection with these tows. States generally also permit their political subdivisions to regulate nonconsensual vehicle towing, often through the ability to impose their own local fee caps or to provide additional consumer protections via local ordinance.

Major stakeholder groups in the towing and motor carrier industries, along with a motorist advocacy group, were contacted in order to obtain their views on nonconsensual towing, the current legal framework, and potential approaches to protecting the rights of motorists whose vehicles are towed. These groups – even those representing towing companies – largely support

State-level consumer protection laws regarding nonconsensual tows. One of the major towing trade groups also suggested that the lingering ambiguity about the potential preemption of State law be removed via Federal legislation that would grant States the right to regulate nonconsensual tows without limitation. Other stakeholders noted problems with the way police-ordered tows are conducted from public ways, with excessive charges for the towing and recovery of heavy vehicles, and with the insufficient protections that some States afford in both of these cases.

The final section of this report summarizes the research and describes potential remedies to strengthen the rights of motorists whose vehicles are towed without their consent. In light of the fact that most States are already enforcing State laws related to trespass towing, one straightforward remedy identified by stakeholders would be simply to delegate, via Federal statute, authority to the States to regulate all aspects of nonconsensual towing. From certain stakeholders' perspective, a major advantage to this approach is that it provides much-needed clarity, eliminating the confusion and uncertainty that has resulted from conflicting court rulings related to preemption. This approach builds on the view that the States are the most logical entities to regulate nonconsensual towing, that they already have an established body of law in place to do so, and that all that is needed is to remove the uncertainties related to preemption. Alternatively, it is suggested that major trade groups in the towing and recovery industry could promote the adoption of a Code of Conduct that would outline the procedures that members will follow when performing nonconsensual tows and would provide guarantees of key consumer protections.

Introduction

Most motorists have had occasion to use towing services for one reason or another. In a typical scenario, a vehicle that has experienced a breakdown or mechanical failure is towed to a nearby garage for repairs. These types of tows are generally referred to as "consensual" tows because the towing is undertaken as part of an agreement between the motorist and the tow operator. Consumers in these cases are free to choose from a number of competing tow services and to negotiate the price and other terms of the contract. (In many cases, consumers may also avail themselves of the services of an automobile club or roadside assistance program to arrange for towing.) Given the substantial consumer sovereignty that motorists can exercise in these cases, prices for consensual tows are generally unregulated.

In some situations, however, the towing of a vehicle can be "nonconsensual," with the vehicle operator having no opportunity to select a towing service or negotiate a rate. As an example, many local police departments have a policy (for safety and operational reasons) of removing wrecked vehicles from roadways using only their own rotational lists of police-approved towing firms. Another type of nonconsensual tow is the "trespass" tow, whereby a private property owner arranges to have an unauthorized vehicle removed from his/her property without the consent of the vehicle owner or operator.[1] Because the motorist in this case is not a willing party to the transaction, nonconsensual tows are often regulated to prevent unfair pricing.

In recent years, a flurry of media attention has raised public awareness of trespass tows and the unfair and deceptive business practices of a relatively small – but prolific – group of "predatory" towing firms. These predatory operators are known to tow vehicles from private property for the most minor of infractions, or in some cases for no infraction at all. They then attempt to hold vehicles hostage until inflated towing and storage rates are paid. In one high-profile case, a pickup truck owned by a church in Hollywood, California, was towed from its own parking lot in the middle of the night; the towing firm asked for more than $1,000 to release the truck and claimed that the church itself had authorized the tow. In another much-discussed case, a vehicle was towed away with a sleeping four-year-old child still inside.

The laws that are designed to protect motorists from these kind of overcharges and abuses involve complex interactions between Federal, State, and local law, and have led to a number of court challenges over the past 10 years. Recently, the legal landscape was changed further by the Safe, Accountable, Flexible, Efficient Transportation Equity Act: A Legacy for Users (SAFETEA-LU), a Federal transportation bill that was signed into law in August 2005. Section 4105 of SAFETEA-LU amended Section 14501(c) of Title 49 of the United States Code with respect to State laws relating to vehicle towing. Specifically, the following language was added to the end of Section 14501(c):

> (5) LIMITATION ON STATUTORY CONSTRUCTION.—Nothing in this section shall be construed to prevent a State from requiring that, in the case of a motor vehicle to be towed from private property without the consent of the owner or operator of the vehicle, the person towing the vehicle have prior written authorization from the property owner or

---

[1] Trespass tows are also known within the industry as "private property impound" (PPI) tows. This report generally uses the term trespass tow.

lessee (or an employee or agent thereof) or that such owner or lessee (or an employee or agent thereof) be present at the time the vehicle is towed from the property, or both.

As subsequent sections of this report will explain in more detail, when Congress adopted amendments to a 1994 Federal law (the Federal Aviation Administration Authorization Act), they permitted tow truck operators to qualify as interstate carriers – exempt from State and local regulation. In addition, less than a year later, Congress adopted the Interstate Commerce Commission Termination Act of 1995, which eliminated the Federal regulatory body that had previously regulated motor carrier rates and services. A provision was included in the bill allowing states to regulate the "price of" nonconsensual tows.

In the years since, a number of conflicting court rulings between towing operators and localities have been issued, which were clarified by the Supreme Court in *City of Columbus v. Ours Garage and Wrecker Service*. The Court found that both State and local governments have the ability to exercise, free from Federal preemption, the "safety regulatory authority" provided in current law. However, the Court declined to address what specific types of regulation would qualify as exercises of safety regulatory authority. Subsequent Federal court decisions have upheld some aspects of local regulations, while staying silent on others.

In addition to allowing States to require written permission or the presence of the property owner for each tow, Section 4105 of SAFETEA-LU also requires the Secretary to Transportation to conduct a study to identify additional means to protect the rights of individuals whose motor vehicles are towed. The Secretary is to submit the findings of this study to the Committee on Commerce, Science, and Transportation of the Senate and the Committee on Transportation and Infrastructure of the House of Representatives not later than 1 year after the enactment of SAFETEA-LU.

Research and analysis for this report was conducted by staff at the John A. Volpe National Transportation Systems Center. Section 1 of the report provides an overview of Federal law related to nonconsensual towing, with particular emphasis on the question of Federal preemption. Section 2 summarizes relevant State laws, and Section 3 presents the views of the major stakeholder groups that were contacted. In Section 4, this material is analyzed to highlight the major issues related to nonconsensual towing and to suggest some potential remedies to the problems identified.

Section 1: Summary of Federal Law Related to Towing

Current Federal law generally "preempts" the regulation of motor carriers, including tow truck operators, by State and local governments. Preemption refers to the displacing effect of Federal law on conflicting or inconsistent State or local laws based on the constitutional principle that Federal law is the "supreme law of the land." Appendix A to this report provides a more detailed explaination of preemption.

1.1   Summary of Legislative History of 49 U.S.C. §14501(c) Relating to Preemption of State and Local Towing Regulation

In 1994, Congress enacted the Federal Aviation Administration Authorization Act (FAAAA) (P.L. 103-305). The FAAAA provided that "a State [or] political subdivision of a State ... may not enact or enforce a law, regulation, or other provision having the force and effect of law related to a price, route, or service of any motor carrier ... with respect to the transportation of property." P.L. 103-305, §601(c) was originally codified as 49 U.S.C. §11501(h), and subsequently recodified as 49 U.S.C. §14501(c)(1). The statute expressly exempted State regulations related to safety, route controls based on the vehicle size or weight or the hazardous nature of the cargo, and financial responsibility requirements. 49 U.S.C. §11501(h)(2)(A), recodified as 49 U.S.C. §14501(c)(2)(A).

According to the House Conference Report accompanying the FAAAA, the legislation was intended, in part, to complete the deregulation of the motor carrier industry and to create a level playing field between the motor carrier and air carrier industries. H.R. Conf. Rep. 103-677, at 85 (1994). The report states that "nothing in [the legislation] contains a new grant of Federal authority to a State to regulate commerce," but also that "nothing in [the legislation] amends other Federal statutes that govern the ability of States to impose safety requirements ... or any other unenumerated authority not preempted by these sections." H.R. Conf. Rep. 103-677, at 84 (1994). It explains that "State authority to regulate safety, financial fitness and insurance, transportation of household goods, vehicle size and weight and hazardous materials routing of motor carriers is unchanged [under the FAAAA] since State regulation in those areas is not a price, route or service and thus is unaffected." H.R. Conf. Rep. 103-677, at 84 (1994). Finally, the report notes that "conferees do not intend for States to attempt to de facto regulate prices, routes or services of intrastate trucking through the guise of some form of unaffected regulatory authority." H.R. Conf. Rep. 103-677, at 84 (1994).

Congress amended and recodified the FAAAA as part of the Interstate Commerce Commission Termination Act of 1995 (ICCTA), P.L. 104-88. The ICCTA added a new exemption to the FAAAA's general preemption rule, allowing States and political subdivisions of States to regulate the price of nonconsensual tows. 49 U.S.C. 14501(c)(2)(C). Further, by specifically employing the term "tow truck," the ICCTA clarified the issue of whether tow trucks are considered motor carriers for the purposes of the statute. The House Report accompanying the legislation explained that the added provision "struck a balance between the need to protect consumers from exorbitant towing fees and the need for a free market in towing services." H.R.

Rep. 104-311, at 120 (1995). The provision was "only intended to permit States or political subdivisions thereof to set maximum prices for nonconsensual tows, and ... not ... to permit re-regulation of any other aspect of tow truck operations." H.R. Rep. 104-311, at 119 (1995).

The ICCTA also added a section providing that "[e]xcept to the extent the Secretary [of Transportation] or [Surface Transportation] Board, as applicable, finds it necessary to exercise jurisdiction to carry out the transportation policy of section 13101 [specifying various aspects of transportation policy], neither the Secretary nor the Board has jurisdiction ... over---(1) transportation provided entirely in a municipality ... or (3) the emergency towing of an accidentally wrecked or disabled motor vehicle." P.L. 104-88, §109, codified as 49 U.S.C. 13506(b). Federal courts have held that this section is consistent with Federal preemption under 49 U.S.C. §14501(c).[2] *See, e.g., R. Mayer of Atlanta v. City of Atlanta*, 158 F.3d 538 (11th Cir. 1998).

On August 10, 2005, SAFETEA-LU was signed into law. SAFETEA-LU added yet another exception to the general Federal preemption of State regulation of towing, this time permitting States to regulate nonconsensual towing of vehicles from private property in order to require written authorization from the property owner or require that the property owner be present before a vehicle may be towed. 49 U.S.C. §14501(c)(5).

The current text of 49 U.S.C. §14501(c) states, in pertinent part, as follows (emphasis added):

> 49 U.S.C. §14501 Federal authority over intrastate transportation
>
> (c) Motor carriers of property.--
>
>> (1) General rule.--Except as provided in paragraphs (2) and (3), a *State, political subdivision of a State*, or political authority of 2 or more States *may not enact or enforce a law*, regulation, or other provision having the force and effect of law *related to a price, route, or service of any motor carrier* (other than a carrier affiliated with a direct air carrier covered by section 41713(b)(4)) or any motor private carrier, broker, or freight forwarder with respect to the transportation of property.
>>
>> (2) Matters not covered.--Paragraph (1)--
>>> (A) shall not restrict the *safety regulatory authority of a State* with respect to motor vehicles, the authority of a State to impose highway route controls or limitations based on the size or weight of the motor vehicle or the hazardous nature of the cargo, or the authority of a State to regulate motor carriers with regard to minimum amounts of financial responsibility relating to insurance requirements and self-insurance authorization;

---

[2] "A similar provision was contained in section 49 U.S.C. 10526(b) prior to the enactment of P.L. 104-88. At least one court stated that on its face that provision indicated Congress's intent not to preempt local towing services." *Interstate Towing Ass'n, Inc. v. City of Cincinnati*, 6 F.3d 1154, 1158 (6th Cir.1993).

...

(C) does not apply to the authority of a State or a political subdivision of a State to enact or enforce a law, regulation, or other provision relating to the *price of for-hire motor vehicle transportation by a tow truck,* if such transportation is performed *without the prior consent* or authorization of the owner or operator of the motor vehicle.

...

(5) Limitation on statutory construction.--Nothing in this section shall be construed to prevent a State from requiring that, in the case of a motor vehicle to be towed from private property *without the consent* of the owner or operator of the vehicle, the person towing the vehicle have *prior written authorization from the property owner* or lessee (or an employee or agent thereof) or that such *owner* or lessee (or an employee or agent thereof) *be present* at the time the vehicle is towed from the property, or both.

In summary, Section 49 U.S.C. 14501(c) provides as follows:

- A State or local authority may not enact a law related to a price, route, or service of a motor carrier.
- A State (or local authority) may enact a safety regulatory with respect to motor vehicles (carriers).
- A State or local authority may enact a provision relating to the price of nonconsensual transportation by a tow truck.
- A State (or local authority) may require in the case of a motor vehicle to be towed from private property without the consent of the owner that the towing operator have prior written authorization from the property owner and/or that the property owner be present at the time of the tow.

1.2 Relevant Federal Court Cases Relating to Preemption of State and Local Towing Regulation

This portion of the report examines court cases concerning the general rule under 49 U.S.C. 14501(c)(1) looking at: (1) consistency with 49 U.S.C. 13506; (2) the statutory prohibition against States enacting laws or regulations related to a price, route, or service of certain motor carriers; and, (3) the market participant exception which allows State and local governments to grant exclusive rights to towing companies to conduct nonconsensual tows from public property. The discussion of court cases also covers judicial interpretations of the safety exception in 49 U.S.C. 14501(c)(2), and the exception concerning the authority of States to enact laws or regulations regarding the price of for-hire motor vehicle transportation by a tow truck when such transportation is performed without the prior consent of the vehicle owner or operator. The report also discusses the new exception (49 U.S.C. 14501(c)(5)) provided by SAFETEA-LU which allows States to enact laws or regulations requiring that, in the case of a motor vehicle being towed from private property without the consent of the owner, the person towing the vehicle must have prior written authorization from the property owner, or that the property owner must be present at the time the vehicle is towed.

1.2.1   General Rule: Consistency with 49 U.S.C. §13506(b)

Federal courts have had numerous opportunities to interpret 49 U.S.C. §14501(c) and other Federal statutes related to towing. Prior to the enactment of the FAAAA, some courts rejected the notion that State and local regulation of towing were preempted by Federal law. In *Interstate Towing Association v. City of Cincinnati*, 6 F.3d 1154 (6th Cir. 1993), for example, a towing trade association challenged a city ordinance requiring that all tow trucks that towed vehicles from locations within city limits to locations either within the city or to locations outside the city be licensed. The plaintiff contended, in relevant part, that the ordinance was preempted by the Interstate Commerce Act, 49 U.S.C. §10521. The court rejected the plaintiff's argument that "Congress ha[d] legislated comprehensively, thus occupying an entire field of regulation and leaving no room for the States to supplement Federal law." The court also noted that the Interstate Commerce Act specifically exempted from Interstate Commerce Commission jurisdiction:

(1) transportation provided entirely in a municipality, in contiguous municipalities, or in a zone that is adjacent to, and commercially part of, the municipality or municipalities, [and]

....

(3) the emergency towing of an accidentally wrecked or disabled motor vehicle.

49 U.S.C. §10526(b). The court concluded that on their faces these subsections indicated Congress's intent *not* to preempt local towing services.

The same language as in 49 U.S.C. §10526(b) is now found in 49 U.S.C. 13506(b), however, the manner in which this language is interpreted has changed since the ICCTA was enacted. In *R. Mayer of Atlanta v. City of Atlanta*, 158 F.3d 538 (11th Cir. 1998), the city of Atlanta adopted several ordinances governing the provision of towing services within city limits. One ordinance made it unlawful for "any person ... to use or operate upon any of the streets of the city a wrecker ... without having obtained a license…" It also made it unlawful for "any person ... to use or to operate upon any of the streets of the city any wrecker without having first filed a registration of all these vehicles with the department of police." The plaintiffs were five towing companies located outside city limits that provided towing services within the city. The issue was whether Federal law preempted the ordinance.

The court first looked at whether tow trucks were covered by 49 U.S.C. 14501(c)(1). The court observed that Federal law defines a "motor carrier" as "a person providing motor vehicle transportation for compensation." *See* 49 U.S.C §13102(12). It concluded that motor vehicle transportation by a tow truck for the compensation of the tow truck company placed the towing companies within the definition of a motor carrier, therefore under the plain meaning of 49 U.S.C. §14501(c)(1), the statute expressly preempted State and municipal ordinances that regulate the prices, routes, or services provided by towing companies. The court found that this conclusion was strengthened by Congress's addition of a limited exemption to the preemptive scope of 49 U.S.C. §14501(c)(1) for nonconsensual towing services, stating that 49 U.S.C. §14501(c)(1) does not apply to the authority of a State or a political subdivision to enact or enforce an ordinance relating to the price of towing services "if such transportation is performed without the prior consent or authorization of the owner or operator of the motor vehicle." See 49 U.S.C. §14501(c)(2)(C). The court noted that if Congress had not intended for 49 U.S.C. §14501(c)(1) to preempt State and local regulation of towing services generally, then it would not have included an express exemption that applies solely to the prices charged for nonconsensual towing services.

The court next looked at whether its interpretation that 49 U.S.C. §14501(c) generally preempted State and municipal ordinances regulating towing was consistent with 49 U.S.C. §13506(b), which provided that:

[e]xcept to the extent the Secretary [of Transportation] or [Surface Transportation] Board, as applicable, finds it necessary to exercise jurisdiction to carry out the transportation policy of section 13101, neither the Secretary nor the Board has jurisdiction under this part over (1) transportation provided entirely in a municipality . . . [or] (3) the emergency towing of an accidentally wrecked or disabled motor vehicle.

The city argued that this section limited the preemptive effect of 49 U.S.C. §14501(c)(1). The court disagreed, concluding that the express reference to towing services in 49 U.S.C. §14501(c)(2)(C) provided conclusive evidence that Congress intended to extend the general rule of preemption to those aspects of the towing industry that were not listed within the exception.

The court also noted that 49 U.S.C. §13506(b) permits the Secretary and the Board to exercise jurisdiction when "necessary . . . to carry out the transportation policy of [49 U.S.C. §]13101." The court observed that the transportation policy of §13101 included the regulation of transportation by motor carriers and the promotion of "competitive and efficient transportation services" and that one of the ways Congress has attempted to carry out this policy was by deregulating certain components of the transportation industry through provisions such as 49 U.S.C. §14501(c)(1). Thus, the court, in finding Federal law preempted the local ordinance, held, enforcement of 49 U.S.C. §14501(c)(1) did not contravene 49 U.S.C. §13506(b) because the exercise of Federal jurisdiction is necessary to accomplish the policy objectives set forth in §13101.

1.2.2   General Rule: Construction of "[R]elated to a price, route, or service of any motor carrier . . ."

Another issue courts examine is whether the State or local regulation is sufficiently related to the price, route, or service of a motor carrier that transports property to be encompassed by the general preemption rule. In *Tocher v. City of Santa Ana*, 219 F.3d 1040 (9th Cir. 2000), the Ninth Circuit held that certain ordinances were related to the price, route, or service of a motor carrier and, thus, were preempted. The city of Santa Ana regulated towing businesses and individual tow truck operators. Towing companies were required to obtain a permit, maintain approved storage facilities, keep certain business hours, obtain written authorization before making consensual tows, notify the police of any nonconsensual tows, provide itemized statements of charges, and publicly display their rates and charges. Tow truck operators were required to obtain an operator's permit, which involved paying a fee and providing information about the applicant's criminal and employment history.

The *Tocher* court noted that a State or local regulation is related to the price, route, or service of a motor carrier if the regulation has more than an indirect, remote, or tenuous effect on the motor carrier's prices, routes, or services. The court observed that the city ordinances in question heavily regulated the manner in which towing companies operated. It reasoned that the regulations erected barriers to entry into the towing business and that those barriers could affect competition for towing services. Further, it stated that the ordinances directly affected the prices, routes, or services of motor carriers, which influenced the relationship between customer and towing operators and indirectly raised costs. Since the regulations had more than an indirect, tenuous, or remote effect on towing services and prices, the court held that there were expressly preempted by 49 U.S.C. §14501(c)(1) unless an exception were found to apply.[3]

In other cases, the Ninth Circuit has held that State towing regulations were *not* preempted because they were *not* sufficiently related to the price, route, or service of a motor carrier. In *Independent Towers of Washington v. Washington,* 350 F.3d 925 (9th Cir. 2003), for example, the court examined a State statute that provided that the last registered owner of an abandoned vehicle was responsible for costs involved with storing and towing that vehicle. The court observed that this statute affected only vehicle owners and did not have even an indirect, remote or tenuous effect on towing companies' prices, routes or service, therefore it was not preempted. In *Tillison v. Gregoire,* 424 F.3d 1093 (9th Cir. 2005), the plaintiff challenged a State statute that, in pertinent part, required towing companies to obtain written authorization from a public official before towing vehicles from public property without the vehicle owner's consent, required the public official to be present for the tow, and prohibited towing companies from serving as agents for public officials. The court concluded that the statue was not related to the price a towing company may charge or the route a towing company may take and that it had only an "indirect, remote, or tenuous effect" on the services a towing company may provide. It went on to hold that even if the statute did regulate tow truck operators' services, it was enacted under the safety regulatory authority of Washington State and, thus, fell within the FAAAA's safety exception.

1.2.3 General Rule: Market Participant Exception

In several cases, Federal courts have held that ordinances granting exclusive rights to towing companies to conduct nonconsensual tows from public property were not preempted on the grounds that the cities enacting the ordinances were acting as market participants, not regulators. In *Cardinal Towing & Auto Repair v. City of Bedford, Texas,* 180 F.3d 686 (5th Cir. 1999), the city of Bedford abandoned its rotational towing system whereby police called towing companies on a rotational basis and passed an ordinance directing that all nonconsensual police tows be handled by the recipient of a contract with the city. The ordinance did not affect consensual tows

---

[3] The court also held that the safety exception to preemption did not apply only because it only exempted safety regulations adopted by State governments, not those adopted by cities. That holding was abrogated by *City of Columbus v. Ours Garage and Wrecker Service, Inc.,* 536 U.S. 424 (2002).

or nonconsensual tows requested by private property owners. A towing company was awarded the contract to handle all police tows within the city. Cardinal Towing & Auto Repair, an unsuccessful bidder, sued the city on the grounds, in part, that the ordinance was preempted by 49 U.S.C. §14501(c). In particular, Cardinal argued that the ordinance constituted regulation related to the price, route, or service of a motor carrier with respect to the transportation of property.

The Dormant Commerce Clause is a legal doctrine inferred from the Commerce Clause of the Constitution, Article I, §8, which grants Congress the power to "regulate commerce among the States." The Dormant Commerce Clause generally prevents States from interfering with interstate commerce, however, States may favor their own citizens when they act as "market participants" and not regulators. In the instant case, the city argued that the ordinance was not a regulation, but rather an ordinary contracting decision of a proprietary nature and, thus, was outside the scope of 49 U.S.C. §14501(c) preemption. The court agreed, concluding that the city's actions were proprietary, reflected the city's interest in the efficient procurement of towing services, and did not constitute the type of regulation covered in the statute's preemption clause. *See also Tocher v. City of Santa Ana*, 219 F.3d 1040 (9th Cir. 2000) (holding that the city of Santa Ana's rotational towing scheme was saved from preemption by 49 U.S.C. §14501(c)(1) by the municipal-proprietor exception to the preemption doctrine; the scheme was established in order to create a reliable list of towing companies who could render quick and efficient towing services for the city).

1.2.4 Safety Exception: Applicability to Local Regulations

One of the most important issues Federal courts have had to address regarding towing issues is whether the safety exception of 49 U.S.C. §14501(c)(2)(A) to the general Federal preemption of towing regulations is available to local governments or only to State governments. In *R. Mayer of Atlanta*, discussed above, the city argued that even if city ordinances regulating towing were preempted under 49 U.S.C. §14501(c)(1), they were nonetheless valid under 49 U.S.C. §14501(c)(2)(A), which excepts regulations adopted under the "safety regulatory authority of a State with respect to motor vehicles" and "the authority of a State to regulate motor carriers with regard to minimum amounts of financial responsibility relating to insurance requirements and self-insurance authorization." While the general preemption, 49 U.S.C. §14501(c)(1), mentions political subdivisions of States, the safety exception, 49 U.S.C. §14501(c)(2)(A), is silent regarding political subdivisions. Observing that a presumption exists that when Congress omits certain language in a particular subsection of a statute and includes the language in other subsections, the omission was intentional rather than accidental, the court held that the city safety and insurance regulations are not exempted from Federal preemption because the exception did not mention political subdivisions. *See also Stucky v. San Antonio*, 260 F.3d 424 (5th Cir. 2001); *Tocher v. Santa Ana*, 219 F.3d 1040, 1051 (9th Cir. 2000) (both holding that local safety and insurance regulations were not exempted from preemption). Parting from the Eleventh Circuit in *R. Mayer of Atlanta*, the Second Circuit in *Ace Auto Body & Towing v. City of New York*, 171 F.3d 765 (2nd Cir. 1999), held that the statute's exemption for "State" safety regulation did not limit the authority of a State to delegate its towing regulatory authority to local or municipal governments.

The Supreme Court settled this division among the Circuits in *City of Columbus v. Ours Garage and Wrecker Service, Inc.*, 536 U.S. 424 (2002). In *Ours Garage*, a towing company sought an injunction to prevent the city of Columbus from enforcing a city ordinance regulating consensual towing. The Supreme Court held that the fact that Congress used the phrase "State [or] political subdivision of a State," in preempting laws enacted by State or their subdivisions relating to price, route, or service of any motor carrier, while it used only the term "State" in stating that this preemption directive "shall not restrict the safety regulatory authority of a State with respect to motor vehicles," was not a sufficiently clear and manifest indication of its intent to preempt local safety laws. The Court reasoned that political subdivisions ordinarily may exercise whatever portion of State powers that a State, under its own constitution and laws, chooses to delegate to the subdivision. Absent a clear statement to the contrary, Congress' reference to the "regulatory authority of a State" should be read to preserve, not preempt, the traditional prerogative of the States to delegate their authority to their constituent parts. Thus, the Court held, 49 U.S.C. §14501(c) does not bar States from delegating to municipalities and other local government units their authority to establish safety regulations governing motor carriers of property, including tow trucks.

1.2.5 Scope of Safety Exception

Federal courts have also struggled with the scope of the safety exception, in particular, what specific types of State and local regulations qualify as exercises of safety regulatory authority such that they are exempted from preemption under 49 U.S.C. §14501(c)(2)(A). In *Ace Auto Body & Towing v. City of New York*, 171 F.3d 765 (2nd Cir. 1999), for example, the Second Circuit construed the safety exception very broadly. New York City had several laws on the books governing municipal towing, including laws requiring tow truck operators to be licensed and establishing qualifications for such licensing. In addition, the city established a rotational towing program and another program granting exclusive towing privileges in certain areas of the city to eliminate the practice of "chasing," in which tow truck operators monitor police radio transmissions to learn of vehicular crash and race to crash scenes. Several New York City tow truck operators challenged the laws on the grounds that the regulations were preempted by Federal law, thus, the issue before the court was the extent to which 49 U.S.C. §14501(c) preempted those regulations.

The court held that the safety exemption in 49 U.S.C. §14501(c)(2)(A) was not limited to safety regulation of the mechanical components of motor vehicles. *See also Tow Operators Working to Protect Their Right to Operate on the Streets of Kansas City v. City of Kansas City*, 338 F.3d 873 (8th Cir. 2003) (declining to undermine the presumption against preempting State police powers by limiting the safety exception to regulations concerning the mechanical components of a vehicle). Further, the court held that city requirements regarding licensing, displaying of information, reporting, recordkeeping, criminal history, insurance, and posting of bond by towing companies, as well as a requirement that tow operators maintain their own storage and repair facilities, were within the safety regulation and financial responsibility exemptions to preemption. The court also held that the city's rotational towing programs were sufficiently safety-oriented to survive preemption. Finally, the court concluded that the statute's exemption for nonconsensual tow rate regulations, 49 U.S.C. §14501(c)(2)(C), applies regardless of the reason for the lack of consent, and thus applies to tows that were nonconsensual solely because the city's rotational system dictated the tower to be used.

The Eleventh Circuit found another far-reaching city regulatory scheme to fall within the safety exception in *Galactic Towing v. The City of Miami Beach*, 341 F.3d 1249 (11th Cir. 2003). In *Galactic*, the court upheld a comprehensive scheme by the city of Miami Beach for licensing and regulating businesses engaged in nonconsensual towing of motor vehicles parked on private property. The ordinance required businesses engaged in the towing and storing of vehicles parked on private property to obtain a permit. In order to obtain a permit, businesses were required to pay an application fee and provide proof of insurance and were subject to a background investigation. In addition, the ordinance made it illegal to tow, remove or store a vehicle except upon the written authorization of the property owner requesting the tow; a blanket authorization made in advance to tow all unauthorized vehicles from a property was not considered valid authorization under the ordinance. Finally, the ordinance required that towed vehicles be stored for the first 48 hours within the confines of the city at an authorized storage facility.

Galactic, a towing company, sued the city, arguing that these provisions were preempted by 49 U.S.C. §14501(c). The city responded that the provisions were enacted to address genuine safety concerns and, thus, that they fell within the safety exemption provided by 49 U.S.C. §14501(c)(2)(A). The city argued, in part, that the purpose of the ordinance was to protect residents and tourists by creating a system of authorized, known tow companies, by eliminating the dangerous practice of crash "chasing," by preventing safety hazards caused by a disabled motor vehicles, by reducing the out-of-jurisdiction time which police officers would have to expend investigating reports resulting from vehicles being towed without the owner's knowledge, and by decreasing the number of disputes over towed vehicles. The issue before the court was whether the challenged ordinance was a safety regulation such that it was excepted from preemption.

The court noted that the Congress's intent behind 49 U.S.C. §14501 was to preempt States' economic authority over motor carriers of property, not restrict traditional State police power over safety. *See City of Columbus v. Ours Garage and Wrecker Service*, 536 U.S. 424 (2002). The court also relied on the legislative intent behind the ordinance. The text of the ordinance stated that the "city commission finds and determines that the unauthorized parking of vehicles that cannot be removed constitutes a public nuisance and a public emergency effecting the property, public safety and welfare of the citizens and residents of the city." Further, the court relied on the unrefuted testimony of city officials, which supported the city's contention that the ordinance was aimed at safety, not economic goals. The court held that the ordinance was a motor safety regulation exempt from preemption under 49 U.S.C. §14501(c)(2)(A), rather than an impermissible attempt to achieve economic goals.

The Fifth Circuit has also upheld requirements for receiving a permit to operate a tow truck. In *Cole v. City of Dallas*, 314 F.3d 730 (5th Cir. 2002), for example, the Fifth Circuit held that a Dallas ordinance prohibiting persons with criminal histories, documented mental illnesses or unsafe driving records from receiving towing permits fell within the safety exception. Cole, the plaintiff, was denied a towing permit based on this ordinance. He filed suit to prevent enforcement of the ordinance, arguing, in pertinent part, that the ordinance did not qualify as an exercise of "safety regulatory authority" under 49 U.S.C. §14501(c)(2). Citing *Ours Garage*, the court noted that Congress' purpose in enacting the statute was to ensure its preemption of States' economic authority over motor carriers, not to restrict traditional State police power over safety. The court observed that the ordinance was adopted to address safety concerns with respect to motor vehicles. In particular, the ordinance's criminal history requirement was designed to curtail confrontations between truck operators and non-consenting vehicle owners. The court concluded that the ordinance had a sufficient nexus to safety concerns to save it from Federal preemption.

In some cases, Federal courts have construed the safety exception surprisingly broadly. In *Hott v. City of San Jose*, 92 F.Supp.2d 996 (N.D. Cal. 2000), a Federal district court held that an ordinance prohibiting intentional fraud on the part of towing companies fell within the safety exception. In *Hott*, the city of San Jose revoked Wanda Hott's tow-car license after determining that her towing firm had intentionally engaged in unlawful, illegal, dishonest, fraudulent, deceitful, and unfair business practices in violation of several provisions of the California Vehicle Code and the San Jose Municipal Code. Hott sued the city, arguing that its regulation of the towing industry was preempted by Federal statute; the city responded that its regulations were authorized by the statute's safety exception. The Court cited the Second Circuit's decision in *Ace Auto Body & Towing*, in which that court found that requirements regarding licensing, the displaying of information, reporting, record keeping, criminal history, insurance, and the posting of bond by towing companies, as well as a requirement that towing companies maintain their own storage and repair facilities, were within the safety-regulation and financial-responsibility exemptions of 49 U.S.C. §14501(c)(2)(A). The court analogized *Hott* to *Ace Auto Body*, noting that the requirements imposed on the tow-truck industry by San Jose were similar to, although perhaps less onerous than, those imposed by New York City. In the end, the court held that San Jose's ordinance prohibiting towing companies from intentionally engaging in fraudulent business practices was not preempted by Federal law as the ordinance was related to safety concerns, not economic interests, and was authorized by State law.

The Ninth Circuit emphasized the importance of the intent behind the State or local regulation in *Tillison v. City of San Diego*, 406 F.3d 1126 (9th Cir. 2005). In that case, a California statute required that towing companies obtain written authorization from the property owner every time a vehicle was towed from his or her property and that the owner be physically present for the actual tow. In effect, this statute made it illegal for towing operators to conduct patrol towing, which involves agreements between towing companies and private property owners under which the towing operator patrols the private parking lots and tows cars that it determines are parked in violation of the parking rules. A towing company sued the city of San Diego, alleging that the statute was preempted by Federal law. The Ninth Circuit previously had held in *Tocher v. City of Santa Ana,* 219 F.3d 1040 (9th Cir. 2000), that a similar California statute addressing patrol towing was preempted by Federal law. After *Tocher*, however, the California legislature amended the statute to clarify that it was safety-related. Noting that the focus of 49 U.S.C. 14501(c)'s safety exception should be on legislative intent and that California had clearly delineated the safety purpose of the provision at issue, the court concluded that the statute was not preempted as it fell within the safety exception to Federal preemption.

1.2.6   Exception for Price of Nonconsensual Tows

In 1995, Congress added an exception to the general preemption rule providing that the general rule "does not apply to the authority of a State or a political subdivision of a State to enact or enforce a law, regulation, or other provision relating to the *price of for-hire motor vehicle transportation by a tow truck,* if such transportation is performed *without the prior consent* or authorization of the owner or operator of the motor vehicle." *See* 49 U.S.C. 14501(c)(2)(C). The Ninth Circuit had the occasion to apply this exception in *Independent Towers of Washington v. Washington*, 350 F.3d 925 (9th Cir. 2003). The State of Washington regulated tow truck operators conducting business within the State, requiring towing operators engaged in nonconsensual towing to obtain permits, submit to inspections of business premises, meet insurance and recordkeeping requirements, maintain certain hours, accept specified means of payment, conform their vehicles to the State's equipment standards, and satisfy other requirements. An organization of tow truck operators challenged the State's regulation of the towing industry on the grounds that it was expressly preempted under 49 U.S.C. §14501(c). The State asserted that the challenged regulations fell within the safety, financial responsibility, and price of nonconsensual towing exceptions to preemption.

The court held that a regulation providing that "[a] registered tow truck operator may receive compensation from a private property owner or agent for a private impound of an unauthorized vehicle that has an approximate fair market value equal only to the approximate value of the scrap in it" was not preempted under 49 U.S.C. §14501(c)(1). Another regulation requiring operators to file fee schedules, forbidding them from charging more than the listed rates, and setting forth procedures for how fees must be calculated was also held not to be preempted because it directly regulated the amount tow operators could recover for their services and therefore was related to the price of for-hire motor vehicle transportation by a tow truck. Finally, the court held that a regulation regulating acceptable methods of payment from customers was not preempted under 49 U.S.C. §14501(c)(1) unless it related to price, however, if the regulation were related to price, then it was saved from preemption under the nonconsensual towing exception of 49 U.S.C. §14501(c)(2)(C). Either way, the court held, the regulation was not preempted. In sum, the court held that several State statutes and regulations challenged were not preempted under 49 U.S.C. 14501(c).

1.2.7   New Exception Under SAFETEA-LU

The SAFETEA-LU added an exception to the general preemption rule providing that the general rule does not "prevent a State from requiring that, in the case of a motor vehicle to be towed from private property without the consent of the owner . . . , the person towing the vehicle have prior written authorization from the property owner . . . or that such owner . . . be present at the time the vehicle is towed . . . " *See* 49 U.S.C. 14501(c)(2)(C). In *Tillison v. Gregoire*, 424 F.3d 1093 (9th Cir. 2005), the plaintiff challenged a State statute requiring, in pertinent part, that towing companies obtain written authorization from private property owners before towing vehicles from private property without the vehicle owner's permission and that private property owners be present while the tow is taking place. The plaintiff, a registered tow truck operator in the State of Washington, conducted patrol and nonconsensual towing of vehicles illegally parked in violation of the statute. The plaintiff sought a declaratory judgment that the statute was preempted by 49 U.S.C. §14501(c)(1). The State argued that the State statute was not preempted because the provisions: (1) were enacted and enforced pursuant to the safety regulatory authority of Washington State, (2) were not related to "route" or "service," or (3) were related to the price of nonconsensual towing. Observing that SAFETEA-LU added another regulatory exception to 49 U.S.C. §14501(c) of the FAAAA explicitly permitting States to regulate nonconsensual towing of vehicles parked on private property, the court held that the State statute was not preempted as to vehicles parked on private property.

Section 2: State Laws and Regulations

This section summarizes current legislation in the States related to nonconsensual towing. Due to resource constraints it was not possible to analyze the statutes for all 50 States in depth. Instead, a sample of nine States, plus the District of Columbia, were selected for further review. This sampling was based on these States' roles in prominent legal decisions and media attention, and was designed to cover several geographic regions of the country.

Because the SAFETEA-LU provision that accompanied the requirement for this report was focused on "trespass" tows from private property, that is also the focus here. Most States have additional towing-related statues that deal with business licensure, insurance requirements, the disposition of dangerous or abandoned vehicles, and the rules governing police-ordered tows from public ways.

2.1 California

Several sections of the California Vehicle Code address issues related to nonconsensual towing in general and to trespass towing in particular. Basic statewide standards for trespass tow operations are set out in Section 22658. This section grants authorization to private property owners to remove unauthorized vehicles from private property "to the nearest public garage" within one hour of notifying the local police, if <u>any</u> of the following are true:

- A tow-zone sign is displayed at all entrances to the property (specific sign dimensions, content, and lettering requirements are listed);
- The vehicle has received a parking ticket and 96 hours have passed since the issuance of the ticket;
- The vehicle lacks an engine, transmission, wheels, or other equipment such that it is not suitable for safe use on the highways; or
- The vehicle is parked on the grounds of a single-family dwelling.

Under Section 22658, the property owner must, wherever possible, provide notification of the details of the tow to the vehicle owner. The code also caps the non-consent tow fee at the rate that would have been applicable for a police-ordered tow in that jurisdiction. Only one day's storage charge is permitted if the vehicle is stored for less than 24 hours, regardless of the number of calendar days. Also, if the vehicle owner returns to the vehicle before it has been towed away, only one-half of the regular towing fee may be imposed.

Of particular relevance to this report is Subsection 22658(l)(1), which states that towing companies may not remove a vehicle from private property without the *written authorization* of the property owner or lessee or their employee or agent, who *must be present* at the time of removal. A blanket authorization to remove vehicles at the towing company's discretion is *not* valid except with respect to vehicles blocking fire hydrants, fire lanes, or entrance and exit. Tow companies towing vehicles under this exception must first photograph the vehicle and later provide a copy of this photograph to the driver when he/she reclaims the vehicle.

Section 22651.1 requires operators of vehicle storage facilities to accept credit cards as payment of towing and storage fees and to have sufficient funds on hand to be able to make change in a "reasonable" cash transaction. This provision was upheld by a California appellate court. Berry v. Hannigan (App. 1 Dist. 1992) 9 Cal.Rptr. 2d 213, 7 Cal.App.4th 587, review denied. Section 21100 grants permission to local governments to pass ordinances regarding regulating the tow truck services whose principal place of business is within the jurisdiction.

With regard to federal preemption, Section 22658 includes a statement of the California legislature's intent to foster public safety via these provisions. As mentioned above, this statement was pivotal in the court's finding in *Tillison v. City of San Diego* that these state laws are safety-related and are therefore not federally preempted.

2.2   District of Columbia (D.C.)

D.C. Official Code, Section 50-2421.03, makes it an offense for any person to park a vehicle on private property without the consent of the property owner. At the same time, Section 50-2421.04 makes it unlawful for "any person, except the [vehicle] owner, a person authorized by the owner in writing, an employee of the District government in connection with the performance of official duties, or a tow crane operator *who has valid authorization from the District government*" (emphasis added) to tamper with or remove a vehicle or attempt to do so.

These two sections, when combined, indicate that a property owner has the unquestioned right to remove an unauthorized vehicle, but that the tow operator may only remove the vehicle once "authorization from the District government" has been received. In fact, this is just what the next portion of the code, §50-2421.05, states (emphasis added):

> The District government or any towing company *at the direction of the Department* shall remove a motor vehicle parked, left, or stored, on private property in violation of §50-2421.03(2) or (3), as follows:
>
>> (1) A vehicle parked, left, or stored without the consent of the property owner shall be removed immediately *after a notice of infraction is issued and conspicuously placed on the vehicle.*
>> (2) A dangerous vehicle shall be removed, with or without the consent of the property owner, immediately after a notice of infraction is issued and conspicuously placed on the vehicle.

Section 50-2421.09 caps tow fees at $100 and storage fees at $20 per day, whether the vehicle was towed by the District government itself or by a private tow company at the direction of the government. (The tow fee is $275 for oversize vehicles requiring special equipment.)

A separate portion of the D.C. Official Code, Sections 50-2421.01 to 50-2421.15, addresses the issue of "abandoned" and "dangerous" vehicles. The District government is authorized to have such vehicles removed from public space (and in some cases private property) at the owner's expense. In the case of dangerous vehicles – e.g. those that are harboring vermin or have exposed glass shards – this can be done without advance warning to the vehicle owner.

In sum, the District's laws regarding trespass towing do not have the same long list of consumer protections as in some States. However, any such tow can occur only after a police officer or traffic control aide has officially ticketed the vehicle for the infraction. Likewise, private towing companies may actually engage in the towing of the vehicle only when acting at the direction of the D.C. government and when the vehicle has been so ticketed.

2.3   Florida

Title XL, Chapter 715, Section 715.07 of the Florida statutes deals with the towing of "vehicles or vessels" from private property. (In this section, boats and other watercraft are treated largely in the same manner as motor vehicles.) It states that property owners have the right to tow away unauthorized vehicles from their property, provided that they comply with the other requirements of this section. These requirements include the following:

- The tow operator must notify the local police (or sheriff) within 30 minutes of the completion of the tow and provide certain details, including a description of the vehicle and its license plate number.
- Towed vehicles must be stored at a site within a 10-mile radius of the point of removal (a 15-mile radius in counties of less than 500,000 population). If no towing business exists within these limits, the 10- and 15-mile limits are doubled.
- Vehicle storage sites must be open from 8 a.m. to 6 p.m. When closed, they must prominently post the phone number where the operator of the facility can be reached, and the operator must return to the site within one hour of a telephoned request.
- Except for single-family residences, tow-away areas must be posted and the signs must meet detailed requirements about size, letter height, and visibility.
- Tow companies must file a complete rate schedule with the local police and post an identical rate schedule at their storage facility. Copies of agreements with property owners (i.e., authorization to tow from their property) must also be posted at the storage site.
- Tow trucks involved in non-consent trespass tows must bear the name, address, and telephone number of the company. There are specific requirements regarding letter height and legibility.
- Vehicle owners have the right to recover their vehicle within one hour of their request. They must be provided with a detailed, signed receipt. They cannot be asked to sign a waiver releasing the tow company from liability for damage as a condition of getting their vehicle back.

A portion of this section (715.07 (2)(a)(4)) also prohibits the granting of money or other valuable consideration in exchange for the privilege of towing vehicles from a particular location. It includes a provision stating that if the vehicle owner (or other authorized person) returns while the tow is in progress and seeks return of the vehicle, the tow operator must stop and return the vehicle provided that a "reasonable service fee" is paid. The service fee is capped at one-half the normal rate for the tow according to the company's published tariff (715.07 (2)(a)(3)).

Importantly, this section also states that these are minimum standards and do *not* preclude the enactment of additional regulations by municipalities or counties. It also explicitly gives municipalities and counties the right to regulate *prices* of trespass tows (715.07(2)(b)). Several local authorities, including populous Broward, Miami-Dade, and Orange counties, have fee caps in the range of $100 for the towing of a typical passenger vehicle from private property.

2.4   Georgia

Section 44-1-13 of the Georgia Code governs nonconsensual trespass tows, setting out some basic principles and empowering the Georgia Public Service Commission (GPSC) to issue and enforce regulations in this area.

In general, the law states that private property owners may have vehicles removed if adequate notice has been posted. However, tow firms and private property owners may not enter into agreements for "automatic or systematic surveillance" of property for towing opportunities, nor may towing companies offer property owners any "fee or emolument" for allowing the firm to tow vehicles from their property. Section 44-1-13 also allows municipalities to impose licensing requirements on the towing and storage firms engaged in trespass tows within their boundaries.

The GPSC has promulgated a number of regulations related to trespass towing, which are listed in Chapter 11 of the Commission's Transportation Rules. First and perhaps most notably, tow firms must obtain a nonconsensual tow permit from the Commission and renew it annually in order to legally transport non-consent tow vehicles over public ways. There are also minimum insurance coverage levels, along with a requirement to maintain three years' worth of detailed records on non-consent tows and to allow Commission representatives to inspect them. The GPSC rules also require that vehicle impound facilities be open at least 6 days per week, be located in the same county as the firm's office (unless authorized otherwise), and be secured, lighted, and locked.

There are specific requirements for the type, size, and content of the notice signs that property owners must place on their property regarding towing. These rules do not apply on residential properties of four units or less. In addition, the GPSC regulations state that nonconsensual tows may not be undertaken without an "authorized contract signed by the owner or other authorized agent" in the form specified by the Commission. In practice, this means that a specific authorization for each tow, not merely a "standing" or blanket authorization, is required. The contract must be made available for the Commission's inspection on request.

Rates for non-consent towing are based on a "Nonconsenual Towing Maximum Rate Tariff," published by GPSC and updated annually. (The rates listed and the annual updates are based in part on input from licensed tow firms on the actual costs of performing the tows.) Tow companies may not impose fees in excess of these maximum rates, nor may they impose storage charges during the first 24 hours or apply additional charges for the use of extra equipment. Storage fees may not be assessed for days on which the storage facility was closed, nor may any fee be imposed once the vehicle has been re-claimed. The storage facility must provide a detailed receipt.

The GPSC regulations also state that if the driver returns to the scene and removes the vehicle before the it is hooked to the tow truck, the vehicle may not be towed and no fee may be charged.

If the driver arrives while the vehicle is hooked or loaded, but has not left the premises, the vehicle must be released. The tow company may collect an "operator's fee," which is also capped by the Nonconsensual Towing Maximum Rate Tariff.

2.5   Maryland

Title 21, Subtitle 10A, Sections 21-10A-01 to 21-10A-06 of the Maryland Code address issues related to the removal of unauthorized vehicles from private parking lots. Parking lots are defined here as facilities with three or more spaces that are open to the public, but where the spaces are intended to be used only for the owner's "customers, clientele, residents, lessees, or guests." This subtitle applies only in the city and county of Baltimore, though it also states that it does not restrict local authorities from licensing or regulating people engaged in the parking, towing, removal, or impounding of vehicles. The basic requirements of this subtitle are as follows:

- Vehicles may not be towed unless there are clear and conspicuous signs warning drivers of the presence of a tow-away zone. The code specifies the required number and size of the signs. The signs must include the following information: the location to which cars will be towed, the price of the tow, and the telephone number for reclaiming the vehicle.
- Vehicles must be taken immediately to a storage facility, which may be no more than 10 miles from the parking lot. The vehicle owner must have an "immediate and continuous opportunity, from the time the vehicle was received at the storage facility" to reclaim the vehicle.
- The tow company must notify the local police within two hours of the tow and provide basic details (vehicle plate number, Vehicle Identification Number, date and time, reason for towing, the tow location, and the storage location).
- The tow company may not impose tow fees more than double the rate charged by the local government for an impound tow, nor impose storage fees of more than $8 per day.
- Tow companies must carry liability insurance and post a surety bond in specified amounts.
- Tow companies may not employ "spotters" (i.e., people tasked with reporting the presence of unauthorized vehicles so that they can be towed), nor may they pay remuneration to the parking lot owner.

Of particular relevance to the present discussion of the towing-related provision in SAFETEA-LU is Section 21-10A-04 of the Maryland Code, which states that the towing company must obtain authorization from the parking lot owner for the tow, including the name of the person authorizing the tow and a statement that the vehicle is being removed at the request of the owner. Although this seems to imply that a separate written authorization is required for each vehicle, it is unclear whether that is the case. It is also unclear whether only the owner himself/herself can give the authorization or if an employee or agent can do so.

A separate section of the code, Section 21-1009, permits the local government of Charles County to "adopt ordinances and regulations relating to the towing or removal of vehicles from privately owned lots."

2.6   Massachusetts

Massachusetts General Laws (MGL), Chapter 266, Section 120D establishes the general right of property owners to have unauthorized vehicles towed away. However, the vehicle operator must be told of the prohibition either directly or via a posted notice. (Unlike the laws in some other States, this section does not specify the necessary wording of the notice or set out any specific requirements with regard to letter heights or legibility.)

For non-consent trespass tows, the property owner must inform the local police and give certain details of the tow (including start and end location and vehicle plate number) *before* conducting the tow. Conducting a trespass tow without either having obtained the consent of the vehicle owner or notifying the police is an offense.

The law requires that vehicles towed away must be stored in a "convenient location," though what constitutes a convenient location is not specified any further. This section also caps the charges for a non-consent trespass tow at the same legal maximum established for emergency tows ordered by police. The charge for storage of the vehicle is also capped at the legal maximum that would apply for storage after a police-ordered tow.

The authority for setting these price caps is set out in a separate section, MGL Chapter 159B, Section 6B, which deals with non-consent tows ordered by the police. This section caps tow fees at a rate to be established by the State Department of Telecommunications and Energy (see below), and caps storage fees at $25 per 24-hour period.

It also states that the fees established apply only to "lighted, outdoor storage facilities enclosed by a secure fence or other secure barrier at least six feet in height." If the storage facility does not meet these standards, the tow company is only entitled to half the rate. This section also requires tow companies to file annual financial reports with the State. It also permits towns and cities to set their own maximum rate for tows within their boundaries, as long as it does not exceed the State maximum.

The actual price limits are established in the Code of Massachusetts Regulations (CMR) at 220 CMR 272.00 and appear to be updated periodically. The current maximum is $90 for up to five miles and $3 per mile beyond that. There are separate provisions and charges related to the towing of commercial vehicles and for any extra labor or special services needed.

2.7   New York

One section of New York State's General Business Laws, Section 399-v, requires parking facility operators to post prominently the name, address, and telephone number of both the parking facility and any person or business authorized to tow vehicles from that facility. In the absence of this required notice, no vehicle may be towed away, and a parking operator who fails to comply with this requirement is subject to a civil penalty of $150.

This section does *not* apply in cities of one million or more, and it also explicitly does not supersede any local laws related to the posting of parking facility notices, as long as these afford "greater protection to the consumer." In combination, these two provisions permit a separate set of rules for New York City (the only city in the State that meets the population requirement).

The New York City Administrative Code, Section 19-169.1, governs the removal of vehicles improperly parked on private property. It includes the following requirements:

- Property owners must conspicuously post signs stating that the area is a tow-away zone and list the name, address, and other details of the tow company.
- Vehicles may not be towed away without the "express written authorization" of the property owner. This authorization must be obtained separately for each vehicle and the written authorization must list details of the vehicle including make, model, color, and plate number.
- Vehicles may not be towed away if they are occupied.
- Vehicle recovery fees are capped at $100 for the tow and first 3 days of storage, plus $10 per day for storage beyond that. (According to the city's consumer affairs office, the allowable storage fee has been raised to $17 per day.)
- Only licensed tow companies can remove vehicles or collect fees of any sort.
- Vehicles must be taken to a storage area within the city limits and (wherever such a facility exists) within 10 miles, and the tow company must notify the police within 30 minutes of the vehicle's arrival in storage.
- If the vehicle driver arrives while the car is "connected" to the tow apparatus, the vehicle must be disconnected and released provided that a "reasonable service fee" is paid. The fee can be no more than one-half the maximum tow fee specified in this section, which would equal $50. Tow drivers are required to carry a copy of these regulations with this section highlighted, and to show it to the driver upon his/her arrival at the scene.
- Vehicle owners have the right to inspect their vehicles for damage before accepting them back from storage. They cannot be obliged to sign any release of liability or similar form as a condition of having their vehicle returned. They must be provided with a detailed, signed receipt.
- No charges can be assessed to the vehicle owner if the tow is not conducted according to these regulations.

2.8 Ohio

Two sections of Ohio's Revised Code address issues related to non-consent trespass towing (a separate set of rules applies for abandoned and junked vehicles). Section 4511.681 makes it a minor misdemeanor to park a motor vehicle on private property without the owner's consent (or in violation of the owner's posted parking guidelines), provided that the property owner has posted a conspicuous notice.

Section 4513.60 allows for two main procedures by which private property owners may have unauthorized vehicles removed from their property. The first, described in division (A) of the section, is relatively simple: after the unauthorized vehicle has been on the property for 4 hours or more, the property owner may contact the local sheriff or police to request removal. The police may then order the vehicle into storage, provided that "whenever possible, [they] shall arrange for the removal of the motor vehicle by a private tow truck operator or towing company." This section applies to residential property (of three or fewer households) and agricultural land.

The other option for Ohio property owners, described in division (B), is to create a "private tow-away zone," in which case unauthorized vehicles may be ordered removed without delay if all of the following procedures are followed:

- Signs are posted at all entrances with the requisite information (including phone number and address of the storage location), meeting letter-size and visibility requirements.
- The vehicle can be recovered "at any time day or night" with proof of ownership and payment of the towing and storage fees.
- Towing fees cannot exceed $90, and storage fees cannot exceed $12 per 24-hour period ($150 and $20 per 24-hours for trucks and buses over 10,000 lbs.).
- The storage/reclaim facility must be "conveniently located" and well-lighted. If the city or town in which it is located has any public transportation service, it must be on or "within a reasonable distance" of a regularly scheduled transit route.
- If the locality requires tow trucks and tow operators to be licensed, only licensed trucks and operators may be used for the removal.
- The local police must be "promptly" notified by the property owner with relevant details of the tow (vehicle plate number, make, model, color, location, date and time, telephone number for reclaim, and storage location).

This division also states that a driver who returns to the scene before the vehicle has actually been removed (but after it has been "prepared for removal") must be given a chance to reclaim the vehicle upon payment of a fee, which may not exceed one-half the charge that would normally apply. The driver must then immediately move the vehicle such that it is no longer on the property or no longer violating the posted regulation, as applicable.

All in all, Ohio's approach appears to go further than other States in facilitating the re-claim of towed vehicles, inasmuch as the police must be notified with all relevant details, the storage facility must be open at all times, and the storage facility must be accessible to public transportation wherever it is available. Although the SAFETEA-LU language would explicitly permit Ohio to require that the property owner or his/her agent provide written authorization for the tow and/or be physically present for the tow, these protections are not part of current Ohio law.

2.9   Texas

In Texas, several different sections of State law, located in the Transportation Code and Occupations Code, address aspects of non-consent towing. Different sets of procedures have been established for different types of private property trespass situations. The law spells out a number of specific consumer protections and provisions, some of which are unique to Texas.

Chapter 684 of the Transportation Code deals with the removal of unauthorized vehicles from parking facilities and roadways. In brief, this chapter states that vehicles may not be towed away from private parking facilities unless adequate notice is given to vehicle owner. Notification requirements are spelled out in detail and include "tow zone" signs with specified minimum letter heights, a notice affixed to the vehicle itself, *and* a notice mailed to the owner of record.

However, there are three exceptions to these requirements: when the vehicle is blocking a vehicular traffic aisle, entry, exit, another vehicle, or a fire lane, or is improperly in a parking space reserved for the handicapped; at a parking facility serving an apartment complex (for which a separate set of rules applies – see below); or when a police officer orders the removal of a vehicle blocking part of a paved driveway or its adjacent entry or exit.

Section 684.0125 of the Transportation Code provides special rules for parking areas serving residential apartment complexes. It prohibits drivers from leaving their vehicles unattended in these parking facilities in a way that obstructs gates or access, blocks a restricted parking area, fire lane, or tow zone, or that "presents a hazard or threat to persons or property." Under this section, property owners and managers may *not* have a vehicle removed simply because it does not bear current vehicle registration plates or inspection stickers (from Texas or another State). Apartment leases and rental agreements to the contrary (i.e., that call for such vehicles to be removed) must provide for the vehicle owner to receive 10 days' written notice; otherwise such lease provisions are void and may not be enforced.

Section 684.014 of the Transportation Code sets out the general rule for towing and storage from a private parking facility, which is that tow companies may *not* remove a vehicle except under the procedures outlined in this chapter, under a conforming municipal ordinance, or at the direction of a police officer or the vehicle's owner. Parking facility operators who arrange to have vehicles towed away in accordance with the other provisions of this chapter (see above) must provide written confirmation to the tow company that the appropriate notice has been given. The parking facility operator must either expressly request that the specific vehicle be removed, or have a standing written agreement with the tow company to enforce its restrictions.

Section 684.105 of the Transportation Code requires tow companies to report towed vehicles to the police within 2 hours. Sections 684.081 and 684.082 prohibit parking facility owners and tow company owners from having financial interests in each other's businesses and from receiving anything of value in connection with the removal of a vehicle.

Section 684.101 of the Transportation Code permits municipalities to adopt ordinances that are identical to those in this chapter or that impose additional requirements. Similarly, Section 643.201 allows municipalities and counties to "regulate the operation of a tow truck to the extent allowed by Federal law" except with regard to truck lighting. Local governments may require registration of tow operators who perform consent tows within their boundaries if the company has a place of business there. They may also require registration of tow companies that perform non-consent tows even if the company does *not* have a place of business there. Municipalities may also require tow operators to obtain a license to perform non-consent tows, but the fee for such permit may not exceed $15.

Sections 643.203-643.204 of the Transportation Code permit localities to regulate the fees that are charged for non-consent tows originating within their boundaries and establish a mechanism for these fee caps to be reviewed via a Towing Fee Study. Localities must adjust the fees "at amounts that represent the fair value of the services of a towing company and are reasonably related to any financial or accounting information provided." Section 643.205 states that if the locality does not regulate non-consent tow fees, then the fee may not exceed 150 percent of the fee that the towing company would be permitted to collect for a non-consent tow ordered by the police.

Section 643.206 of the Transportation Code requires towing companies to take vehicles only to licensed storage facilities and to charge only the storage fees permitted by Chapter 2303 of the Occupations Code (see below). Sections 643.207-208 require tow companies to file their *non-consent tow fee schedules* with the Texas Department of Transportation on an annual basis and to post these schedules at their vehicle storage facilities in view of the consumer.

Chapter 2303 of the Occupations Code makes general provisions for operators of "vehicle storage facilities," including the requirement to obtain a license for this activity. Section 2303.155 sets maximum allowable fees, including a $50 cap on notification fees, $20 for impoundment, and daily storage fees not to exceed $20. Fees other than those spelled out in the law are not permitted.

Under Section 2303.158 of the Occupations Code, operators of vehicle storage facilities are required to accept debit and credit cards for all transactions related to vehicle storage. This section also requires storage operators to allow customers to have access to the vehicle's glove compartment or console in order to retrieve documents that would prove their identity or their ownership of the vehicle.

2.10   Virginia

The Virginia legislature recently passed legislation related to trespass towing. This section summarizes the existing statutory framework as well as the recent changes that have been made.

The Code of Virginia, Section 46.2-1231, states that private property owners may remove unauthorized vehicles from their property, but only if conspicuous signs are posted at the entrances to the parking area warning motorists of the fact that vehicles parked there without permission may be towed or immobilized. It also requires tow truck operators to report such tows to the local police and for tow companies to prominently display their fee schedule. Charges in excess of the posted rates are not permitted.

This section also states that if the vehicle owner arrives in time to remove his/her vehicle before the tow, the vehicle cannot be towed. In this situation, the towing company may however demand a fee of up to $25 "in lieu of" towing. Counties, cities, and towns can set a different fee by local ordinance.

Sections 46.2-1232 and 46.2-1233 state that counties, cities, and towns may pass ordinances regulating non-consent trespass tows and may set "reasonable limits" on towing fees for trespass tows, "taking into consideration the fair market value of such removal." In doing so, however, the locality must take guidance from a local advisory board that includes appointed representatives of law-enforcement, towing and recovery operators, and the general public (Section 46.2-1233.2).

If no local fee cap has been adopted, a statewide cap of $85 or $95 applies to trespass tows of passenger vehicles. The higher fee is applicable if the tow takes place on a weekend or holiday or between 7 p.m. and 8 a.m. (Section 46.2-1233.1). This section also states that no storage charge is permitted for the first 24 hours.

These provisions were amended by a recently passed bill, SB 134, which raises the cap on non-consent tow fees to $125 ($150 for evenings, weekends, and holidays). Localities can continue to impose different caps within their jurisdictions.

Among its other changes, SB 134 requires towing and storage facilities to accept at least one major national credit card for payment and requires that "tow zone" notice signs include the local non-emergency police telephone number or the telephone number of the tow company. The legislation prohibits certain financial relationships between tow companies and property owners. It also grants local authorities more discretion to regulate non-consent trespass tows, including the ability to require photographic evidence to justify a tow, the ability to impose additional notice and signage requirements, and the ability to require "second signatures" from property owners (or their agents) prior to the tow.

Also noteworthy is the fact that SB 134 creates a new 15-member State "Board of Towing and Recovery Operators" to license and regulate the towing industry and tow operators. The board will have representatives from State government, the towing and recovery industry, and the general public. It will set and enforce licensing standards and will have the power to revoke licenses for noncompliance. The Board will also receive complaints from citizens and establish procedures to mediate disputes between towing firms and their customers. Although it is too early to tell what impact this Board will have, the intent was to create a "watchdog" agency that would work with the towing and recovery industry to curb abuses and enhance consumer protection.

2.11 Summary

As outlined in Section 1, prior to the passage of SAFETEA-LU, States' ability to regulate nonconsensual trespass towing was primarily limited to matters related to safety and to the price of such tows. The language in SAFETEA-LU expanded this scope slightly to include the ability to require that the property owner (or his/her agent) provide written authorization for each tow and/or be physically present.

In spite of this arguably narrow mandate, each of the States reviewed for this section has an extensive regulatory scheme related to nonconsensual trespass towing, with a range of consumer protections and other provisions. Table 1 below highlights the similarities and differences in these State laws, with the most typical provisions listed first. These include requirements about the posting of notices on private property, the establishment of price ceilings on towing and storage charges, requirements for police notification, and regulations on the location and operation of the vehicle storage and reclaim facilities used in connection with these tows.

Each of these States also permits its political subdivisions to regulate towing in at least one respect or another, often through the ability to impose their own local fee caps or to provide additional consumer protections via local ordinance. Though not quite as common, most also have some provision for allowing the driver to reclaim his vehicle – without it being towed – if he/she arrives before the vehicle has been removed and can pay a service fee.

The requirement for specific written authorization and/or presence of the property owner, the subject of the SAFETEA-LU language, is somewhat less common. It is used in several States, including California, which is the home State of one of the representatives who sponsored the amendment. Some other less typical provisions include bans on constant surveillance or the employment of "spotters" and bans on financial ties or the giving of consideration between property owners and tow companies.

The approach taken in the District of Columbia is notably different from the States reviewed. Its law includes relatively few specific consumer protections (e.g. regarding notice signage, release fees, financial ties, and the like), but it does require that the vehicle be officially ticketed for the trespass parking offense prior to towing. This would presumably sharply curtail the kind of "predatory" or "patrol" towing that has been discussed in media accounts and by consumer groups, but at the expense of property owners' ability to remove vehicles quickly. It may be that this approach is more suitable for urban areas where traffic control aides and parking enforcement officers can more readily issue a ticket.

Table 1: Comparative Overview of State Towing Laws

Provisions of State Law	California	D.C.	Florida	Georgia	MA	Maryland*	New York*	Ohio	Texas	Virginia
Signage/notice requirements at entrances to private property	✓		✓	✓	✓	✓	✓	✓	✓	✓
Cap on tow and/or storage fees	✓	✓		✓	✓	✓	✓	✓	✓	✓
Police reporting requirement	✓	✓	✓		✓	✓	✓	✓	✓	✓
Regulations on size, proximity/location, and/or hours of storage facility	✓		✓	✓	✓	✓	✓	✓		
Localities may impose own requirements or fee caps	✓	n/a	✓	✓	✓	✓	✓	✓	✓	✓
Provision for mandatory release of vehicle if driver arrives prior to tow	✓		✓	✓			✓	✓		✓
Ban on financial ties or payments between property owners and towers			✓	✓		✓			✓	✓
Specific authorization and/or presence of property owner or agent required for tow	✓			✓		✓	✓			
Storage facility must accept credit card(s)	✓								✓	✓
Storage facility cannot require waiver of liability as condition of release			✓				✓			
Ban on surveillance or "spotters"				✓		✓				
Vehicles may be towed only after police issue notice of violation		✓								
Certain lease provisions regarding towing unenforceable									✓	
Requires non-consent tow permit from State				✓						

* Maryland law applies only in the city and county of Baltimore. New York law includes some statewide provisions, but the information in this column refers principally to New York City regulations.

Section 3: Stakeholder Views

In this section, the views expressed by stakeholder groups are summarized and discussed in relation to the findings of the previous sections. The groups contacted represent a range of organizations active in issues that affect the motor carrier and towing industries, as well as major players in the market for towing services.

3.1 Towing and Recovery Association of America

The Towing and Recovery Association of America (TRAA) is a trade group that represents the interests of members in the towing and recovery industry. The authors of this report held a teleconference with TRAA staff (including the president and executive director, along with several other employees and members) and received a "position paper" on non-consent towing from their attorney. A copy of the position paper is included here in Appendix B.

According to TRAA, its members already abide by numerous State and local laws regulating trespass towing. Most local tow operators accept State and local regulation as an inevitable part of doing business in this field, even though it creates additional complexity and operational constraints. In its position paper, the TRAA stated that "towers from around the country have never understood the hoopla over [preemption] because they have abided by strict State or local laws that have fully regulated private trespass towing for years."

TRAA staff and attorneys, on the other hand, are quite familiar with the Federal preemption issue. They believe that in at least some instances, a strong case for Federal preemption of State laws could certainly be made. For example, TRAA questions whether requirements that specific types of notice signage be posted or that credit cards be accepted are really "safety" issues.

Interestingly, however, rather than re-visit the preemption issue, TRAA would prefer to *remove the ambiguity about Federal preemption* once and for all by amending Federal law to allow States to regulate trespass tows without reservation. They provided proposed statutory language that would accomplish this, and which is presented in Appendix B.

In their view, the current situation – including the SAFETEA-LU language – is undesirable because it gives States the unambiguous right to regulate trespass tows in only a few particular ways and not in others that might be more effective. In its members' experience, requiring written authorization or the presence of the property owner can cause security problems, for example by giving rise to potential confrontations with intoxicated motorists. Rather than permit States only a handful of particular legislative approaches, they would rather have the States be given free rein to regulate this area in ways that truly respond to local needs and circumstances.

In our discussion, TRAA members also stated their opinion that the *State* level is the best arena for setting legal price ceilings for nonconsensual tows. Their members say this because (1) attempting this at the national level would be impractical and would make it difficult to account for differences in local labor and equipment costs, and (2) local governments often do not have the resources to conduct the kind of cost and market studies that would be required to set a reasonable rate.

TRAA members are also very concerned that the focus on trespass towing *not* become a stepping-stone to the idea of States' re-regulating regular consensual towing services. In their view, this would be clearly contrary to Congress' intent and to the spirit of de-regulation, since with consensual tows the consumer is a willing marketplace participant. TRAA members also note that their profit margins are being squeezed by the combined market power of automobile clubs and roadside-service programs, along with rising fuel prices, so State regulation of their consensual tow rates would further compromise their economic viability.

With regard to excessive towing charges for heavy vehicle recovery – an issue raised by the trucking industry – TRAA acknowledged that abuses can sometimes occur, but pointed out that States already have the power to regulate prices. The association expressed an interest in reaching out to the trucking industry to work together to reduce overcharges.

3.2   National Towing and Recovery Association

The National Towing and Recovery Association (NTRA) is also an industry association representing the interests of towing and recovery operators. The authors spoke with William (Bill) Johnson, who is both the chairman of the NTRA and the head of its Massachusetts chapter. Mr. Johnson noted that NTRA shares the public's concerns about the abuses that can occur with "patrol" towing from private property. He also pointed out that even well-designed laws governing trespass towing need to be matched by proper implementation by the local police, citing cases from Massachusetts where town police misunderstood the details of State law.

Mr. Johnson also solicited comments from individual NTRA members and shared these with us. The comments received reinforce the idea that tow operators already work within the constraints of State and local laws related to trespass towing, and that these laws are not an undue imposition. In fact, two of the commenting NTRA members said that for their own protection, they take additional steps to ensure that trespass tows are properly authorized. One firm requires the property owner to be present and takes pictures to document the situation, while another requires a separate written authorization from the property owner for each tow.

One NTRA member noted that the towing industry receives "overly negative media coverage that seems to condone illegal parking." The TRAA position paper presented in Appendix B (see discussion above) also sounded this theme, noting that discussions of trespass towing often do not fully consider the rights of property owners to control access to their property.

With regard to the provision in SAFETEA-LU permitting States to require the presence and/or written authorization of the property owner for a trespass tow, the NTRA comments generally express a belief that it was a step in the right direction. One commenter called the provision a "good thing" and suggested that we should "see how it works."

3.3   American Towing Alliance

The American Towing Alliance (ATowA) is a nationwide network of towing operators that offers its services to trucking fleets. Their goal is to provide reliable, cost-effective towing and recovery services for their clients. The authors spoke on several occasions with Chris Carlson, their Chief Operating Officer, and Gay Rochester, a transportation incident management specialist at ATowA. The discussions focused on heavy vehicle towing, as their organization has relatively little connection to private property trespass tows.

One of ATowA's primary concerns is with the tow rotation lists used by State Departments of Transportation and local police departments for removing wrecked vehicles from public ways. The Alliance believes that in many cases there is inadequate oversight of these lists and that insufficient attention is paid to keeping unscrupulous firms and unqualified personnel off the lists. Conversely, they also believe that in some cases DOTs impose excessive equipment requirements on tow operators as a condition of participating in the rotation program. These requirements serve as barriers to entry to the market, causing prices to rise.

State highway authorities are focused on clearing the scene of highway crashes quickly in order to prevent additional traffic congestion. Therefore, they often insist on using their tow-rotation systems rather than allowing motor carriers to use the tow company of their choice because of a concern that this would lengthen the clearance time. ATowA staff told us that what can happen, however, is that the rotation tow firm will send unnecessary equipment and staff to the scene and will not work as expeditiously as possible in order to maximize the per-hour vehicle and equipment charges that can legally be levied. This is due in part to the fact that there is no ongoing business relationship between the motor carrier and the towing firm, and thus no incentive for the tower to nurture this relationship via competitive pricing.

Like the other groups in the towing industry, ATowA is aware of the Federal preemption issue but largely considers this a footnote to the fact that many States do regulate this area extensively via State law and regulations. Recently they worked to help pass legislation in Virginia (see Section 2 above) that provides additional oversight of the towing industry. Ms. Rochester stated that, in general, the State level is the appropriate one for regulating towing, but that they are concerned about what to do in States that do not have effective rules. In particular, they believe that State laws often fail to provide consumer protections to drivers of heavy commercial vehicles, as opposed to passenger automobiles. ATowA plans to send additional written comments on this topic.

3.4   American Automobile Association

The American Automobile Association (AAA) is a consortium of regional automobile clubs that provides a wide variety of automotive and travel-related services to its members. AAA is a major player in the consensual towing market by virtue of its roadside assistance service, which uses a nationwide network of tow contracts to dispatch help to AAA members. The organization also uses its large size to negotiate competitive towing rates. We spoke by telephone with the association's legislative and public affairs officer in Washington, D.C., who indicated that his statements reflected the general sense of AAA but were not "official" positions.

Generally, AAA deals only with consensual tows, where the consumer is free to choose from competing services, thus making for a very different transactional relationship with the tow operator than is the case with nonconsensual tows. Therefore, AAA would like to ensure that any regulation of nonconsensual tows does not (inadvertently or otherwise) spill over into consensual tows, where the market can operate effectively without statutory price controls.

This caveat notwithstanding, AAA views itself as an "advocate for motorists" and supports legislation to protect consumers from the abuses that can occur with predatory trespass towing. AAA cited provisions requiring adequate warning signage and imposing price ceilings on trespass tows as two examples of common-sense consumer protections.

In some cases, AAA members do not have the opportunity to use the AAA roadside assistance towing provider in the case of a freeway breakdown because a tow is ordered by police as part of a "quick clearance" program. The organization prefers that members be allowed to use the tow service of their choice, but when this happens, they are usually able to work with the member to provide reimbursement.

3.5   Owner-Operator Independent Drivers Association

The Owner-Operator Independent Drivers Association (OOIDA) is a membership organization for independent truck drivers. In addition to serving as an advocacy group on trucking-related policy and legislative issues, OOIDA provides direct member services such as insurance, financing, group discounts, and administrative support.

The authors held a conference call with three senior members of OOIDA (including their treasurer and general counsel) to discuss their organization's views on nonconsensual towing. OOIDA noted that they had already been in touch with Congressional staff on this issue. OOIDA's main concern is not with "predatory" or "patrol" towing from private parking areas, although in some cases this affects their members, but rather with the exorbitant towing fees that unscrupulous tow operators charge for towing and recovery of OOIDA members' vehicles from public rights-of-way.

When OOIDA drivers are involved in highway crashes or breakdowns, they often do not have a meaningful choice regarding which towing and recovery company to employ, either because they are in an unfamiliar area of the country, or because the tow is ordered by police using a rotation system. In some of these cases, after conducting the service the tow company presents an excessively high bill – many times more than the actual fair market value of the towing services rendered – and holds the driver's truck "hostage" until this bill is paid. Owner-operators faced with this situation typically have little choice other than to pay the charges – their truck is their livelihood and their deliveries are time-sensitive. OOIDA, through its insurance arm, does however contest some of the most egregious overcharges and in several instances has taken towing companies to court to recover excessive towing fees. It is their experience that these abusive practices on the part of tow operators have "increased radically" over the past few years.

OOIDA believes that there is insufficient oversight of this area, as there is no Federal regulation and in some cases no State-level regulation of these towing charges. While some States do impose price ceilings on nonconsensual tows (see Section 2 above), the complex nature of towing and recovery operations for heavy commercial vehicles – which often requires special equipment and additional labor – makes it difficult for legislators and regulators to set an exact price cap in dollar terms. Instead, there may be a cap for passenger automobiles but no cap for heavy vehicles, or the cap for heavy vehicles may be expressed in dollars per hour of labor. These approaches leave room for abuse.

In their view, the SAFETEA-LU language does not go far enough in protecting their members' interests, because it deals only with vehicles towed from *private* property without the consent of the vehicle owner. Almost all of their problems stem instead from tows from public ways. (As noted in Section 1, however, rotational towing schemes and the accompanying price ceilings have generally been upheld by Federal courts as falling within a proprietary or "market participant" exception to the general rule of Federal preemption of State law.)

OOIDA staff stated that some form of national oversight of this issue would "solve a lot of problems" for their members. In general, they prefer uniform national rules rather than State and local ones; anti-idling laws and engine-braking laws are examples of other areas where they struggle to stay abreast of a changing patchwork of State and local laws. States and localities could also be more careful about which tow companies make it onto their rotation lists.

3.6   American Trucking Associations

The American Trucking Associations (ATA) is a trade group that represents the interests of the trucking industry. The authors spoke by telephone with a staff attorney for ATA who is familiar with this area. It was stated that the primary concern of ATA and its members is the exorbitant bills for towing and recovery services that truckers sometimes receive in connection with police-ordered tows from public ways. Like some other stakeholders, ATA is somewhat dissatisfied with the rotational towing schemes in place in some localities and with the inability of State regulatory schemes to keep prices in line with the actual market value of the services rendered. ATA indicated that it is not uncommon for tow operators to send unnecessary equipment to the scene and to take extra time to complete the work in an attempt to justify a high towing bill.

Private property trespass towing is an issue that has received less attention at ATA, but it is also not unheard of for a commercial driver to have his/her vehicle towed as part of a "predatory" or "patrol" tow. ATA acknowledged that States already have the ability to regulate the prices of nonconsensual tows – through the "marketplace participant" exception to Federal preemption in the case of police-ordered tows, and through the specific statutory exemption in the case of private trespass tows. Therefore, any legislative remedy would likely be at the State rather than the Federal level.

3.7   American Highway Users Alliance

The American Highway Users Alliance is an advocacy group that seeks to improve the safety and mobility of the Nation's highway transportation system. A legislative affairs officer stated that the Alliance has no official position on this issue and declined to offer any informal input.

Section 4: Discussion

The mandate for this report comes from a requirement in SAFETEA-LU that the Secretary of Transportation conduct a study:

(a) To identify issues related to the protection of the rights of individuals whose motor vehicles are towed,
(b) To establish the scope and geographic reach of any issues so identified, and
(c) To identify potential remedies for those issues.

The preceding sections of this report have addressed parts (a) and (b) via a review of Federal and State laws related to nonconsensual towing and consultation with major stakeholders. Together, this information identifies the legal avenues that are available to individuals whose motor vehicles are towed without their consent (particularly from private property), the issues and complexities that have arisen in this area of law, and the scope and geographic reach of these issues.

In this section, this information is analyzed in further detail to address part (c), that is, to identify potential remedies for the issues that have been raised. As a starting point for this discussion, it may be useful to separate the issues that have been raised in the preceding sections into three general areas: issues with the legal framework, practical concerns for motorists, and concerns of the towing industry.

4.1   Issues With the Legal Framework

As described in Section 1, Federal legislation has created a situation in which, with a few exceptions, State regulation of the prices, routes, or services of towing operators is federally preempted. While this is not necessarily problematic in itself, several issues have arisen that have created difficulty for individuals seeking legal recourse under their State laws.

First, even after numerous court cases and a Supreme Court appeal, there is lingering ambiguity about the scope of the safety exception to Federal preemption. In several cases, provisions that might seem to a reasonable observer to be safety regulations were overturned as a pretext for economic regulation, while the reverse has arguably been true in other cases. The language in SAFETEA-LU has given States another means of regulating nonconsensual tows, but does not address the ability of States to provide other forms of consumer protection that may be more valuable. (It also does not address the problems that can arise with police-ordered tows of vehicles from public ways.)

Another major concern with the current legal framework is that most States regulate nonconsensual towing in numerous ways (and, at least by their own accounts, most tow companies abide by these laws) without much regard to the subtleties of preemption doctrine. Many State regulations are enforced unless and until they are successfully challenged in court. Meanwhile, although the Federal Government claims primacy in this area (except for those aspects over which States have been granted permission to regulate), there is no agency or office within the Federal Government that takes an active role in promoting consumer protection in towing-related cases. This complex pattern of interaction between Federal, State, and local laws has created confusion among towers and consumers alike and has restricted the ability of vehicle owners to pursue legal claims.

Finally, one more specific challenge associated with the legal regulation of nonconsensual towing is that it may be difficult (though by no means impossible) for legislators to devise a meaningful price ceiling for the towing and recovery of heavy commercial vehicles. This is because unlike passenger cars, there are many factors that affect the costs involved, as well as different types of specialized equipment that may be required for certain types of tows.

4.2   Practical Concerns for Motorists

Motorists' concerns about nonconsensual towing are well-known and have received much attention in the media. Many of the problems stem from the fact that the vehicle owner is not taking part in a voluntary transaction; he or she is instead being billed for services ordered and rendered by others. As a result, one of the main problems relates to high and unpredictable tow fees, particularly in areas of the country where such fees are not strictly regulated.

A related set of concerns relates to the so-called predatory aspects of trespass towing, including constant surveillance of parking areas, collusion between property owners and towers, and the towing of vehicles for the most minor of infractions. In some cases, vehicles are towed for no real reason at all, including cases where phony signage (quickly put up and taken down) is used to "document" violations.

Other dishonest or questionable business practices include refusing to release a hooked vehicle even when the driver returns to the scene and offers to remove it; refusing to give receipts or itemized bills; holding vehicles hostage; making it difficult to reclaim vehicles and/or holding erratic business hours; refusing to accept any form of payment other than cash; and damaging vehicles in transit. In the worst cases, "bad actors" use physical intimidation, particularly in the unwelcoming environment of the impound lot, to extort additional money from customers. Safety issues have also arisen, both in the general case where a driver is left stranded at night, and in particular cases where vehicles were towed while they were still occupied.

4.3   Industry Concerns

In discussions with representatives of the towing industry, it is clear that the current system presents issues for them as well. For one thing, they believe that local governments tend to establish ceilings on nonconsensual tow rates without sufficient input from the industry or hard data on the actual costs of performing these tows. Another concern is that the patchwork of State and local laws can make it difficult even for conscientious towers to play by the rules. Finally, a number of tow operators expressed concern that additional State regulation of nonconsensual tows could become a "foot in the door" for re-regulation of regular consensual tow services.

4.4   Potential Remedies

In discussions with stakeholders, the remedies suggested most frequently involved an element of delegating additional authority to States to regulate nonconsensual towing. Section 4105 of SAFETEA-LU is one move in this direction, in that it gives States the right to regulate two particular aspects of trespass tows. However, several stakeholders pointed out that this provision does not address tows from public ways and that it is insufficient (or undesirable) to permit only these two specific forms of consumer protection. The provision also does not resolve the underlying legal ambiguities about Federal preemption of State laws on trespass towing, consumer protection, and fraud; it might even be argued that it only reinforces the general rule of Federal preemption by enumerating additional exceptions.

4.4.1 New Federal Legislation

In light of the fact that most States (at least in the more urbanized areas of the country) are already enforcing State laws related to trespass towing, one straightforward remedy mentioned by stakeholders would be simply to delegate, via Federal statute, authority to the States to regulate all aspects of trespass towing. A slightly more expansive option would be to delegate this authority with respect to *all* nonconsensual towing, including both trespass tows and police-ordered tows. This second approach is precisely what was suggested by the TRAA (see Appendix B for their proposed statutory language).

From certain stakeholders' perspective, a major advantage to this approach is that it provides much-needed clarity, eliminating the confusion and unpredictability that has resulted from conflicting court rulings related to preemption. This approach would firmly establish the State (along with its political subdivisions) as the proper venue for crafting and enforcing laws that balance the rights of vehicle owners, property owners, and tow operators. In addition, consumers seeking redress for overcharges or other unfair treatment would no longer be in the Catch-22 position of having their State case thrown out on preemption grounds only to find that they may have no real recourse at the Federal level either. Since business practices and towing costs vary from place to place, it may also be more practical to have nonconsensual towing regulated by the States rather than by the Federal Government. This approach builds on the view that the States are the most logical place to regulate nonconsensual towing, that they already have an established body of law in place to do so, and all that is needed is to remove the cloud of preemption.

A variant of this approach would be to delegate the necessary authority to the States via statute, but then to require that each State regulate nonconsensual tows in some substantive way that protects motorists. This would address the concerns of some stakeholders that they are vulnerable to predatory practices in States that do not control these tows. Because in our Federal system States ordinarily cannot be outright compelled to legislate in this way, this approach would require some sort of Federal incentive to comply, possibly coupled with the drafting of "model" legislation to be adopted.

4.4.2 Options Within Current Policy Framework

From a pragmatic viewpoint, it is also important to consider remedies that can be implemented even in the absence of any changes to Federal law or policy. One might argue that the *status quo* allows States to provide an acceptable level of consumer protection, inasmuch as States already have substantial leeway – via the market participant, safety, price, and other exceptions to Federal preemption – to regulate nonconsensual tows. One option would be to keep this policy framework in place while additional, voluntary measures are implemented by the towing and recovery industry. For example, working through their trade associations, the major towing companies could agree to a

Code of Conduct that would outline the procedures that members will follow when performing nonconsensual tows and would provide guarantees of key consumer protections. The code could include a provision for arbitration of consumers' grievances (without affecting their rights to seek redress via the legal system). Meanwhile, within the Federal Government additional research on existing Federal consumer protection statutes might also be able to identify provisions that could be relevant to motorists with complaints against towing operators. This would provide them some recourse in cases where their State claims are prevented due to preemption, yet would not require a new Federal program or office.

Appendix A: Background on Preemption

Preemption refers to Federal law's displacing effect on conflicting or inconsistent State or local laws. Under the Supremacy Clause of the United Stated Constitution, the laws of the United States are "the supreme Law of the Land . . . any Thing in the Constitution or Laws of any State to the Contrary notwithstanding." Art. VI, cl. 2. While the Constitution does not mention municipalities, "for the purposes of the Supremacy Clause, the constitutionality of local ordinances is analyzed in the same way as that of statewide laws." *Wisconsin Pub. Intervenor v. Mortier,* 501 U.S. 597, 605 (1991). The Supreme Court has held that State and local laws are preempted where they conflict with the dictates of Federal law and, consequently, that they must yield to those dictates. *See Gibbons v. Ogden,* 22 U.S. 1, 210-11 (1824). On other occasions, the Court has declared that State laws that are found to conflict with Federal law are simply "without effect." *Cipollone v. Liggett Group, Inc.,* 505 U.S. 504, 516 (1992).

Preemption "may be either express or implied, and is compelled whether Congress' command is explicitly stated in the statute's language or implicitly contained in its structure and purpose." *Morales v. Trans World Airlines, Inc.,* 504 U.S. 374, 383 (1992). It occurs in three different circumstances: (1) when Congress enacts a statute that explicitly preempts State law; (2) when State law conflicts with Federal law; and (3) when Federal law occupies a legislative field to such an extent that it is reasonable to conclude that Congress left no room for State regulation in that field. *Cipollone v. Liggett Group, Inc.,* 505 U.S. 504, 516 (1992). Whether a Federal statute preempts a State or local law depends on the Congress' intent in enacting the statute. *Cipollone v. Liggett Group, Inc.,* 505 U.S. 504, 516 (1992) (noting that Congressional intent is the "ultimate touchstone" of preemption analysis). *See also Ace Auto Body & Towing, Ltd. v. City of New York,* 171 F.3d 765, 771 (2nd Cir.1999), *cert. denied,* 528 U.S. 868 (1999).

Preemption analysis "start[s] with the assumption that the historic police powers of the States [are] not to be superseded . . . unless that was the clear and manifest purpose of Congress." *Medtronic, Inc. v. Lohr*, 518 U.S. 470, 485. *See also N.Y. State Conference of Blue Cross & Blue Shield Plans v. Travelers Ins. Co.,* 514 U.S. 645, 654 (1995). Police powers refer to the rights and powers reserved to the States by the Tenth Amendment to pass laws regulating public health, safety and welfare. Further, the Court has held that even when it is clear that Congress intended to preempt State regulations, the scope of the preemption is determined by the statute and must be tempered by this presumption against preemption. *Medtronic, Inc. v. Lohr*, 518 U.S. 470, 485 (1996). *See also City of Columbus v. Ours Garage and Wrecker Service, Inc.,* 536 U.S. 424, 432 (2002); *Cipollone v. Liggett Group, Inc.,* 505 U.S. 504, 517 (1992). In such cases, "analysis of the scope of the preemption statute must begin with its text." *Medtronic, Inc. v. Lohr,* 518 U.S. 470, 484 (1996). In assessing the scope of Federal preemption, courts also look to the statute's legislative history and to regulations promulgated pursuant to the statute. *Scurlock v. City of Lynn Haven*, 858 F.2d 1521, 1523 (11th Cir.1988). For example, in determining whether particular State or local towing regulations are preempted, courts have held that because Congress expressly preempted certain aspects of towing and the Federal statute "provides a reliable indication of Congressional intent, the issue of preemption must be resolved by determining whether the . . . [Federal statute] . . . encompasses the state/local regulations" at issue. *See Tocher v. City of Santa Ana*, 219 F.3d 1040, 1045-46 (9th Cir. 2000). On the other hand, "Congress' enactment of a provision defining the preemptive reach of a statute implies that matters beyond that reach are not preempted." *Cipollone v. Liggett Group, Inc.*, 505 U.S. 504, 517 (1992).

Appendix B: Written Comments Received from Stakeholder Groups

Peter B. O'Connell

Attorney at Law
130 Washington Avenue
Albany, New York 12210
Ph: (518) 436-7202 FAX: (518) 436-7203
e-mail: peter.oclaw@verizon.net

April 10, 2006

Mr. Sean Peirce
Volpe National Transportation
 Systems Center
55 Broadway
DTS-42
Cambridge, MA 02142

RE: PREDATORY TOW TRUCK OPERATIONS STUDY

Dear Mr. Peirce:

As you know, I am counsel to the Towing and Recovery Association of America (TRAA). I am also counsel to Empire State Towing and Recovery Association, which is a statewide towing association in New York and the Coalition of Northeastern Towing Associations, which is a coalition of towing associations from 13 northeastern States. My clients' position with respect to the so-called "Predatory Tow Truck Operations" study is as follows:

Although it is an issue that is beyond your control, my clients take umbrage to the title of the study because it paints an entire industry with a brush that should be applied to a miniscule few. Indeed, the incident that precipitated the Cox-Moran amendment to HR-3 involved the accidental towing of a vehicle from a shopping center with an infant aboard. Who is to say that this would not have occurred if the owner of the shopping center was present at the time of the tow? Cox-Moran is yet another example of allowing a dramatic – although extremely rare – incident to serve as the catalyst for making bad law.

THE PROBLEM WITH COX-MORAN

Cox-Moran provides statutory guidance that allows States to prohibit "patrol towing" (i.e., the towing of vehicles from private property without specific authorization from the owner of the property). It was intended to reverse a court decision that found a California law that prohibited patrol towing to violate the ICC Termination Act of 1995.[4] Although well-intended, Cox-Moran deprives property owners of the right to effectively control access to their property. Five examples may serve to illustrate this point:

---

[4] The case was subsequently reversed by the 9th Circuit Court of Appeals; *Tillison v. City of San Diego, 406 F3rd 1126 (9th Cir. 2005)*

- Many property owners (particularly those that are located near bars or fast food establishments contract with towing companies to patrol parking lots at night because they are scattered with food wrappers, broken beer bottles and other detritus on a daily basis.
- Many homeowners (particularly those who reside near sports stadiums, beaches and other tourist attractions) contract for patrol towing because they are routinely denied access to their property.
- Since 9-11, many facilities (particularly governmental buildings) contract for patrol towing for security purposes.
- Many shopping centers and residential complexes contract for patrol towing to clear fire lanes and other sensitive areas.
- Businesses often contract for patrol towing because their patrons cannot gain access to their property.

In essence, Cox-Moran provides that these property owners must provide a half-hour of free parking (the time that it generally takes to dispatch a tow truck) to trespassers who often damage their property, provide security threats, or deprive them of the ability to earn a livelihood.

Although the 9th Circuit decision in *Tillison* found that the California laws that prohibit patrol towing promote safety, arguments that arrive at a contrary conclusion are equally as compelling. For one thing, it does not appear that the Court addressed issues involving the large number of intoxicated motorists[5] who engage in private property trespasses. A ban on patrol towing not only invites parking lot confrontations with these individuals but it facilitates their return to the highways. From a purely legal point of view, the major problem with the Appellate Court's decision in *Tillison* is its failure to balance its shaky findings on safety against the private property rights that are violated by trespassers.[6]

PROPOSED ALTERNATIVE TO COX-MORAN

Despite our misgivings with *Tillison* and Cox-Moran, we do recommend changes to Federal law that will serve to more fully protect the rights of both governmental agencies and consumers. In essence, 49 USC §14501 only allows States to enact laws that are based upon considerations of safety and to regulate the *price* of towing that ". . . is performed without the prior consent or authorization of the owner or operator of the motor vehicle." In reality, a tow without prior consent (generally referred to a "nonconsensual" tow) applies only to tows that are either authorized by a police officer (or other governmental official that is authorized to cause the removal of a disabled, abandoned or illegally parked vehicle) or an owner of private property.

There are, however, aspects of nonconsensual towing that are not based upon considerations of safety and price that should be regulated. Accordingly, we recommend that States and political subdivisions of States be provided with authority to regulate *all* aspects of nonconsensual towing. This may be accomplished by repealing the Cox-Moran amendment (paragraph (5) of subdivision (c)

---

[5] Some towers estimate that more than half of the nighttime private property trespassers are intoxicated.

[6] The trial court, on the other hand, found the law to be ". . . an economic regulation" that makes it "more difficult for a private property owner to protect a valid property right."

of 49 USC §14501) and by amending sub-paragraph (C) of paragraph (2) of subdivision (c) to read as follows:

> (c) does not apply to the authority of a State or a political subdivision of a State to enact or enforce a law, regulation or other provision relating to the [~~price of for hire motor vehicle transportation by a tow truck, if such transportation is performed without the prior consent or authorization of the owner or operator of the motor vehicle~~] <u>towing and storage of a motor vehicle when such towing and storage is authorized by a police officer or other person designated by such State or political subdivision to cause the removal and storage of a motor vehicle or by the owner or lessee of private property from which the motor vehicle is removed.</u>

Among other things, this amendment codifies many of the court decisions that have come down since the enactment of the ICC Termination Act that have served to regulate nearly every aspect of nonconsensual *police* towing. The more sweeping of these decisions find the adoption of rotation lists and other methods of responding to police calls to be a "proprietary function" of a State or political subdivision that falls outside of the preemptive provisions of §14501.[7] Other decisions allow municipalities to enact laws that prohibit "chasing" to accident scenes.[8]

One aspect of police towing that has not been fully litigated in the courts involves a determination as to whether a tow is consensual or nonconsensual. In this regard, it has been argued that a police authorized tow becomes consensual (and, thus, unregulated) if a motorist is able to sign for a tow at an accident scene. The proposed amendment removes this ambiguity in the law.

The amendment is of greater value in the "private trespass" (i.e., towing of vehicles from private property) arena. Towers from across the country have never understood the hoopla over Cox-Moran because they have abided by strict State or local laws that have fully regulated private trespass towing for years. Although these laws are rarely challenged, it is most likely many aspects of them would be struck down because they fall outside of the scope of the safety exception to §14501.

For example, it is a slight stretch to argue that a requirement to accept a credit card is related to safety.[9] It is even more of a stretch to argue that the posting of "no parking – towaway zone" signs is related to safety. Laws that regulate private trespass towing also cover such non-safety related issues as the tower's hours of operation, reclamation policies, parking lot security, and distance from the site where the vehicle was removed. Most of them also require a tower to notify a local police precinct whenever a vehicle is removed from private property. The proposed amendment protects these, and other, aspects of well-established private property trespass laws from court challenge.

Having represented the towing industry for over 25 years, I find that a fairly large number of complaints relate to the *price* of nonconsensual police authorized tows. Although the vast majority of

---

[7] *Petrey v. City of Toledo, 246 F3rd 549 at 559 (6th Cir. 2001)* and *Cardinal Towing and Repair, Inc. v. City of Bedford, Texas, 180 F3rd 686 (5th Cir. 1999).*

[8] *Ace Auto Body and Towing, Inc. v. City of New York 171 F3rd 765 (2nd Cir.1999)*

[9] The trial court in *Tillison* did, however, find such a provision to be related to safety.

disputes involving price are resolved on the side of the tower, there are occasional examples of over-billing - particularly on heavy duty accident recoveries, which, due to equipment and manpower requirements, can often run into the thousands of dollars. The aggrieved parties, however, are generally well-heeled trucking or insurance companies that are fully capable of taking care of themselves in court. More importantly, Federal law already provides States with complete authority to regulate these prices. If there is a failure to provide adequate protection from overcharging on police authorized tows, it is a failure of State – not Federal – law.

Complaints involving private trespass tows generally fall into three categories: "I didn't see the sign; I was only there for a minute; and I can't believe it cost so much." As explained above, there is already a mature body of law on the State level that deals with these issues, - which laws would be insulated from court challenge through our proposed amendment.

Although Congressmen Cox and Moran won't want to hear this, the biggest problem with most local private trespass towing laws is that they are overly onerous to towers. Most municipalities don't even have private trespass laws because towers who engage in this business – particularly in smaller communities – do so in a responsible manner. After all, the person whose car you just towed might be a customer or a neighbor.

When a local government enacts a private trespass law it is generally because a tower has abused the process. To illustrate, I know of one local law that was enacted because a tower was charging $400.00 per tow. When this occurs, the local government reacts with a sense of retribution and enacts a law that is so stringent that no responsible tower will want to go into the business. These laws generally contain rate schedules that are clearly confiscatory[10] and other features that render it impossible to maintain a profitable private trespass business. Contrary to the title of your study, consideration should also be given to protecting towers from the actions of predatory municipalities.

CONSENSUAL TOWING

Although the focus of the "Predatory Towing" issue seems to be centered on private trespass towing, the wording of the mandate for a study is broad enough to cover other aspects of the towing industry. The towing industry's greatest fear with the study is that it could lead to the reversal of hard-fought gains on the "consensual" tow side of the equation. Enactment of the ICC Deregulation Act of 1995 spawned numerous lawsuits that challenged local laws that regulated consensual towing on the grounds that they were not based upon considerations of safety.[11]

Stripped to their essentials, most of these laws serve no public purpose but to add revenues to local coffers. One of the more egregious examples is New York City, where, until recently, it was unlawful to merely drive a tow truck through the City or to enter the City for the purpose of picking up or dropping off a customer's vehicle without obtaining a bi-annual license that costs more than

---

[10] Such a practice violates the ICC Termination Act. The sponsor of the Act, Congressman Bud Shuster of Pennsylvania, stated the following: "I would note that with the restoration of the authority of local units of government to regulate prices to be charged for nonconsensual towing, the Congress fully expects that any rates so established be compensatory and reasonable." *Congressional Record at page H15600*

[11] e.g., *Harris County Wreckers Ass'n v. City of Houston, 943 F.Supp. 711 (S.D. Tex.1996)*

$600.00 per truck. This law was struck down by a Federal District Court Judge on March 24, 2006 on the grounds that it violates the so-called "dormant" Commerce Clause of the U.S. Constitution.[12]

The chilling effect that local laws such as this has on commerce is exactly what Congress intended to cure when it enacted the ICC Termination Act. The problem is even more acute when neighboring municipalities enact conflicting and often retaliatory local laws. To illustrate, an *amicus brief* filed by TRAA in the *Ours Garage* case revealed the following:

> One of the many examples of such multi-jurisdictional towing companies is the business run by TRAA's Treasurer, Charles H. Schmidt, Jr., based in the village of Roslyn, in the Town of North Hempstead, New York. Mr. Schmidt operates a fleet of eight tow trucks, employs four drivers, and pays license fees in 13 different jurisdictions totaling over $4000 per year. And even though his base of operations is within 10 miles of New York City, Mr. Schmidt elects not to obtain a license to pick up vehicles within the City due to the added cost and burden of New York's licensing program.

The exorbitant cost of abiding by these laws is, of course, passed along to the consumer.

Aside from reducing these regulatory burdens, the primary purpose of the ICC Termination Act was to rid the trucking industry (which includes towing) of tariffs and to allow the dynamics of the marketplace to control the cost of these services. Since most of the local laws that plagued Mr. Schmidt and others in the towing industry originated as forms of price control, many of them have either been struck down or fallen into disuse because there is no longer an economic justification for their existence.

Which brings us to another central question: i.e., should State and local governments be allowed to, once again, regulate the price of consensual towing services? Without being overly dramatic, it is most likely that such re-regulation would result in widespread business failures within today's volatile towing market – which is already in serious decline as the result of ever-increasing fuel, insurance, employee and equipment costs.

Although percentages vary from business to business, I estimate more than 80 percent of today's towing industry is already subjected to some form of economic regulation. This regulation takes the form of municipally mandated police towing and private trespass rates and participation in motor clubs, vehicle warranty programs and long-term contracts with customers. In all of these instances, towers are unable to unilaterally adjust their prices to accommodate such factors as constantly fluctuating fuel prices. Municipalities and motor clubs, in particular, are extremely slow in reacting to these market forces and they rarely provide the degree of relief that is necessary for towers to remain financially viable. Re-regulation of what remains of the consensual towing market would only exacerbate this problem.

---

[12] *Automobile Club of New York, Inc. v. City of New York, 04 Civ. 02576 (RO) (S.D. NY, 2006)*

The small consensual market is also extremely competitive. When regulated tows (described above) are taken out of the equation, the only tows that remain are those that result from Web site, yellow page or other advertising – and most persons seeking these tows are shopping for price – and tows that are solicited at breakdown or accident scenes – an activity that could be curtailed if a municipality chooses to do so.

Given the foregoing, it is safe to conclude that re-regulation of consensual tows would result in substantial harm to the industry and virtually no benefit to consumers.

Thank you for the opportunity to respond to this study and please do not hesitate to contact me if I can provide additional information. I look forward to our conference call on Wednesday.

Sincerely,

Peter B. O'Connell